SAME SAME BUT
DIFFERENT

A soul approach to mental health - Book 1

Marie
ANT✳INETTE
El-Helou

BALBOA.PRESS

A DIVISION OF HAY HOUSE

Balboa Press books may be ordered through booksellers or by contacting:

Balboa Press
A Division of Hay House
1663 Liberty Drive
Bloomington, IN 47403
www.balboapress.com.au
AU TFN: 1 800 844 925 (Toll Free inside Australia)
AU Local: (02) 8310 7086 (+61 2 8310 7086 from outside Australia)

Print information available on the last page.

ISBN: 978-1-9822-9608-7 (sc)
ISBN: 978-1-9822-9609-4 (e)

Balboa Press rev. date: 11/04/2022

Testimonials

Working with Marie has changed me. It's changed my relationship with my family and friends, the world around me, but most of all, my relationship with myself. I've gained a deeper understanding of who I am, why I have experienced things in my life, how to learn from them and how to move forward to carry out my mission in this life.

Marie has a deep understanding of other worlds, inner worlds, outer worlds and other dimensions and how healing can come about working with all of these! She helped me understand boundaries within this physical world and the non-physical and how my lack of boundaries has led to a lot of suffering in the past. I finally feel I can have compassion, deep understanding and love for myself and my journey so far, and it feels very freeing.

Most of all, I'm very thankful because I'm not scared anymore. I don't let fear run my life, thanks to Marie. I highly recommend her to anyone looking for a non-judgemental, kind and empathetic mentor to help you to see the true power and potential within you.

MERRYN B

I have known Marie for over seven years. I met her when I was trying to make a big decision and had become stuck. She took no time to let me know that I already knew what I was going to do and encouraged me to find confidence in my future path. I was so impressed by her reading – not only for her psychic insights but for her skills as a therapist and ability to understand my perspective and thoughts. I have maintained my connection with Marie and have consulted her several times when I have reached a stalemate or crossroads in my life. She never fails to offer solace, humanity, and an uncanny ability to comprehend my dilemma and the issue at hand – with the overriding understanding that I have free will to make my own choices. I always come away from our sessions having learned something about myself and with energy and enhanced confidence to look afresh at my situation and make a well-informed decision. Marie never fails to stun me with her spiritual and psychic ability – she is truly amazing.

JUDY O'ROURKE

I have been working with Marie for about five years now and I have to say she is one of the most gifted healers I have had the pleasure to work with.

Marie gets down to the core of your issues and clears them with such ease and unconditional love. She's very relatable and makes you feel so comfortable with her energy and humour.

Marie adds insight when you are in need of further clarity and she does it with such a loving energy and it's very evident in the way she communicates that she genuinely wants to help people. I was also blessed to be able to take part in her 1:1 Intuition Ignition mentoring program in 2018 which helped me clear multiple blocks and fears as well as tap into my own intuitive abilities which has paved the way for me to start my own business as an energy healer. I highly recommend Marie, she is truly a gift and has made such a great impact in my life.

KALPANA PATEL

I have had the pleasure of being in a creative circle with Marie and witnessing her natural healing abilities. After the first I had an overwhelming feeling like Marie had opened something inside me that was missing, and in another, it can only be described as an explosion that went right through my soul. I felt such emotions that had built up and finally released. I can't thank Marie enough for awakening my entire being and helping me understand the person I always knew I was deep inside. I now look forward to the journey and continued guidance from such a spiritual soul that is Marie.

FIONA DEAN

Marie was such a wonder to work with; she created such a beautiful space which I felt totally safe in. Marie intuitively guided me through a starseed activation which was something out of this world, next-level stuff. I would recommend Marie to everyone who has that little voice in their head.

RHYS MCKAY

I was extremely fortunate to meet Marie when I did. In many ways I was aware of what was happening for me at the time, but Marie pinpointed an issue that needed to be addressed and helped me understand why particular events in my life had occurred and what I needed to do to move on from old negative experiences. I found that Marie was able to help me get in touch with the core essence of my being in a way that no other healing practitioner has before. I feel Marie would be a great asset to anyone looking to grow spiritually and get to the bottom of their major life issues.

BEAUMONT MILES

I have been doing some healing sessions with Marie quite recently. For me I have experienced a lot of trauma in my life and always felt stuck in life not knowing who I am or what my purpose in life was. Since I've met Marie, I have been able to shift a lot of unconscious baggage & blocks, release past life attachments, let go of family beliefs & discover answers about myself. She is one of the most compassionate, caring, knowledgeable and experienced practitioners I have ever come across and is spot on with everything she does. Her techniques and skills are so effective and quick it has given me so much relief from a lot of things that have been holding me back in my life. I really enjoy working with Marie and would recommend her to anyone who is looking at changing their life, belief patterns and looking for answers.

JO WATT

When I first found Marie's Intuition Ignition Program, my business was struggling and my access to intuitive guidance was very blocked, to say the least. I was very hesitant at first to try the Intuition Ignition Program but eventually decided to give it a go and thank goodness I did. Marie helped me heal a limiting belief I was holding onto around money and time. She also helped me clear up beliefs around being worthy of receiving divine guidance and its possibilities for me. My business is now back on track and functioning very successfully again. And my access to intuitive guidance has opened up beautifully now and has become a very natural process in my life. I cannot be more thankful to Marie and her program.

AVIN PRASAD

From the first time I met Marie I knew she was gifted, but it wasn't until having a one-to-one session that I realised that there is a lot more to her. Healers I have been to in the past do the healing, but I had no idea what happened and why I was experiencing everything that I was and left with questions. What I love about Marie is she holds a safe space, takes time to allow you to understand what you've been experiencing and explains the healing process. My heart is always full of gratitude after a session with her.

She is also a talented MC and comedian. After having Marie MC at my Embody Your Rawness event, I knew I would get her back as an MC and to speak at The Wild Ones Live, a two-day event. Marie can have the room laughing one moment and deep in thought the next.

She has so much wisdom, an endless supply of jokes and walks the talk. You know you have nothing to worry about when she is around; she creates a unique and memorable experience for your guests. It's always a pleasure to have Marie.

AMANDA J. MCKAY

I have been working on and off with Marie for 5 years. Our first shamanic session set the stage for a powerful awakening and healing journey. After years of addiction and other mental health issues I thought I was going mad, yet I was opening a door to the spirit world and a deep purging of my soul which I couldn't have got through without Marie's help. Marie's ability to express herself with clarity, guidance, clear messages, and tough love at times from her, the other realms and dimensions has saved my life. I hold Marie in the highest regards. As a now friend and fellow soul traveller Marie is my first port of call when things arise that are beyond my ability to see, hold and express. Her swift intuitive skill of reading energy with eagle eye precision is without parallel. I can't thank Marie enough for saving my life and showing me the gifts and talents that have lay deep within my soul just waiting for the right person to unlock and activate. I highly recommend Marie to anyone willing to go deep within their soul to find the truth of who they are.

JULES UTICHI

To all of those who have ever felt different to everybody else, who have been labelled, suppressed, felt crazy, weird, isolated and alone, this is for you. Blessings to you; may you find solace, wisdom, relief, humour and inspiration within.

Sensitive Souls who Behave Differently (SSBD)

Contents

Prologue   **xvii**
   Meet the Co-authors   xviii
Introduction   **xxiii**
The Key of Acceptance   **1**
   Super Sensitives   2
   Empaths   4
   Taking on Illness   6
   The Clairs   9
   The Pleiadians on Acceptance   11
The Key of Awareness   **15**
   Non-physical Entities   15
   The Other Side of the Veil   17
   Positive Effects   18
   The Sceptic   19
   Negative Effects   21
   The Pleiadians on Awareness   26
   Protection Affirmation   29
The Key of Awakening   **31**
   Existential Crisis   35
   It's Time to Grow Up!   36
   Spiritual Awakening   38
   The Dark Night of the Soul   39
   Ego Loss   41
   Spiritual Emergency   44
   Kundalini Awakening   45
   The Pleiadians on Awakening   47
The Key of Vibration   **51**
   The Real Dangers   52
   Psychic Centres   54
   Other Extra-curricular Activities   55
   Co-morbidity   56
   Grounding   58
   The Pleiadians on Addiction   59
   The Ashtar Command   62

The Key of Consciousness   **65**
The Superconscious Mind   68
Trauma   69
A Shamanic Perspective   74
Soul Fragments   76
The Soul Retrieval Process   77
The Modern-day Experiencer   78
Maat's Perspective on Consciousness   79

The Key of Divinity   **83**
Family Constellations   87
Past Lives   89
Starseeds   91
The Pleiadians on Starseeds   92
Keepers and Seekers – The Starseed Calling   94
Divine Intervention   95

The Key of Ascension   **99**
The Galactic Federation of Light   99
Ascension   101
From 3D to 5D   103
Ascended Masters   104
The Pleiadian View on Ascension   106
Planetary Ascension   110

The Key of Truth   **113**
Truth with Self and Others   115
Projection   116
Personal Power   118
Beliefs   120
The Biggest Illusion of All   121
The Pleiadians on Truth   123

The Key of Perspective   **129**
The Soul Lens   130
Super Powers   133
The Pleiadian Perspective   134
Anxiety   136
Psychosis   138

The Key of Alignment   **143**
I Am That I Am   143
The Universe is Always Listening   147
Metatron   149

The Key of Forgiveness   **155**
    Radical Responsibility   156
    Resentment   158
    Ho'oponopono: I Love You, I'm Sorry,
    Please Forgive Me, Thank You   158
    The Pleiadians on Forgiveness   160
The Key of Harmony   **165**
    The Goddess Kali   165
    The Divine Feminine and Masculine   168
    Non-Duality   169
    Money and Love   171
    The Goddess Kali on Harmony   172
Afterword   **179**
Acknowledgements   **181**
About the Author   **183**
Recommended Reading List   **185**
Program Offers   **187**

Prologue

My first visit to a psychiatric ward was when I was about seven years old. My father had taken me there to visit my mother. The best way to describe my mother was that she was severely depressed. When she wasn't constantly wanting to sleep and die, she was staying awake and ranting non-stop in a way that made no sense. As we waited in the corridor for one of the nurses to go and fetch her from her room, I remember feeling anxious as I looked around and saw people in various states of consciousness. There was some yelling going on in the distance and it sounded like it was getting louder. The yelling was from a lady wheeling herself down the corridor in a wheelchair. She was shouting that she knew the truth and what the governments were really doing, that they were trying to kill us all. I remember her looking at me directly in the eye when she said, "They don't want us to live, they want us to die ... and because I know the truth they are going to come now and shut me up with their injections."

And sure enough, three men came running down the corridor, one injecting a needle into her arm while the others violently held her in place, even though she couldn't run. Her screaming rapidly declined as she slumped into her chair. I remember feeling upset, helpless and that I couldn't do anything to stop this. Deep down somewhere in that little body of mine, I felt that she was speaking the truth and I wanted to know more. Visits to the hospital were frequent in the following years to see my mother and later my brother. I was always fascinated by the other patients, their stories and their beliefs. I often felt a deep curiosity about how they reached such states, coupled with a growing resentment of what I saw as their 'treatment'. It felt like a prison where they doped people up to their eyeballs to manage them.

I became deeply passionate about how our world views mental health, with a strong suspicion that as a society, we somehow had it all wrong. Little did I know, even after I began formulating ideas for this book over ten years ago and established a career in mental health, that I too would be speaking the 'truth' and some men in white would be coming to not only inject me but throw me in a padded cell; that I would be told I was just like my mother and had inherited bipolar disorder through her genes. They were wrong and right. Same same but different. I did inherit something from her, yes, but it wasn't bipolar disorder!

Years later, not long after my first psychiatric admission after 'they' told me I was disordered and feeling traumatised by the idea that I just might be, I came home and heard a very loud and distinct voice. It was in Arabic and the words spoken were: "Do not be afraid". It was my grandmother. She proceeded to tell me that I came from a long line of incredibly psychic women and that I also possessed these skills. She warned me that unless I learnt to understand and use these skills wisely, I would end up in the revolving door of the mental health system. She was right.

Meet the Co-authors

This book is only half written by me. But before I introduce you to the co-authors, I want to share with you the unfoldment of how I've come to this collaboration.

In 2009, I started writing to God. Inspired by Neale Donald Walsch, who wrote the series of books *Conversations with God*, I thought I would have my own conversations and, lo and behold, I began getting answers. It was clear that the responses were not from me, and I have to say they were quite comical; I found God to be quite the smart-arse! I really enjoyed retreating into this world, so kept up the writing until one day I got a response in plural form: "We would like you to know ..."

I was flabbergasted (love that word) and when I asked, I was given the initials M and G, with no other information. For months I would wonder, till one day I had a flashback to a time when I was extremely distressed and suicidal in my late twenties. I was contemplating leaving this world when I began to have flashes of my life shown to me. Similar to *Footprints in the Sand*, they all seemed to be flashes of challenging times in my life; but in the memories there were two big-winged angelic figures next to me and they telepathed that they had been assigned to be with me, and would always be with me, never leaving my side. Then I remembered that several spiritual healers had told me they had felt archangels Michael and Gabriel around me, and I was like, "Cool – that's who those big bad-ass angels were!"

"Why the mystery?" I exclaimed to them in my next sitting, and they said they were here to empower me, not spoon-feed me, and it was important I find my own answers.

My writing continued, and again there was a change in tone. I was asking who it may be, but no spoon-fed answer came. One morning, I woke up with the word 'Metatron' in my head on repeat. I had no clue what this meant; maybe some European car ... I mean, I liked cars and was in the market for one, but no – I found out that Metatron was on the ascended master level of beings, so I didn't get the new car but an upgrade into a higher realm instead!

Metatron and I struck up a great friendship and I learnt a lot until, less than a year later, the answers to questions began to say 'we' again. At first I thought the archangels were back, but I noticed I was getting much bigger-picture information about the world, and the tone changed to one that was comical and ironic. I showed a friend one day and she said my writings were remarkably similar to Barbara Marciniak's work in which she channelled an advanced extra-terrestrial (ET) race called the Pleiadians.

I can't really explain the full extent of how I felt when I read her channelled writings, because I instantly knew – the tone was the same, even some of the phrases, their straightforwardness and humour, there was no doubt about it – I had been in dialogue with the same crew. With the realisation that I had been upgraded yet again, I also had an unmistakeable feeling as though I was finally coming home!

This book will take you through a journey of 12 keys, rather than chapters. Each key has a part written by someone or some group from my spiritual team. I have been told that these channelled messages are encoded with a frequency designed to awaken your spirit and liberate your soul just by reading them. I use the word 'channelled' for a sense of ease, but the process is more like mediumship, where I am just speaking on behalf of a group of elders on topics I know well in my soul memory.

My 'team' consists of enlightened beings and ascended masters including the Pleiadians. The Pleiadians are our distant cousins who have achieved not only personal ascension, but a planetary one. They hold a lot of advanced information on humanity. They as a collective have come to be like a group of mates who have always got my back and are ready to answer anything I ask. To give you a heads-up, the Pleiades is a seven-star cluster visible in our night skies, and its origins trace back to every ancient indigenous culture around the world, known as the tale of the seven sisters. In Australia, the stories associated with the stars and night skies carry deep meanings embedded in Aboriginal law, culture and social structures of the most ancient of human civilisation.

After I began my journey with the Pleiadians, they often accompanied me outside of writing and showed themselves to me in my mind's eye several times, and I began to remember. As my soul memory awakened, it was shown to me that I had done most of my growing up as a soul in this star system. Now that explained why I felt like I was an alien all my life! They explained that they were my ancestors from the stars and that they were the ones who dropped the idea in my head that I would be writing a book. Three, in fact! They showed me what all the Mayan prophecies were about and said it was important to explain the ongoing ascension process, because the world would see many great changes happening and the ascension process could have lots of people thinking they were crazy.

You would think that the rest is history and that this is where I finally wrote the book you have in your hands. If you remember *The Karate Kid* or have seen *Peaceful Warrior*, you might recall the frustration that the characters went through. Nothing was explained and they had to learn via mysterious experiences with a lot of 'what the fuck is this about', and they came to a point where they had to defeat their own personal demons to overcome some adversity. Welcome to my world! As mentioned before, it turns out my experience required more 'research' of the firsthand kind. I needed to experience my biggest fear imaginable: the men in white coats with syringes in hand.

So, there I was, writing a book about mental health, and suddenly I found myself on the inside of the system, experiencing firsthand the degradation, humiliation, labelling and rejection from friends and family. It was a real eye-opener. Seeing the irony in my situation, I tried to tell the doctors that I was a psychotherapist myself and understood what had happened to me. To lighten things up, I cracked a joke and then mentioned that I was a comedian. I didn't expect to be stared at like some freak and totally ignored. I later found out why when I obtained my file notes under the *Freedom of Information Act*. There, in black and white, it said:

Patient is suffering a delusion that she is a psychotherapist and a comedian.

But wait, there's more. Another two hospital 'stays' followed over a difficult seven-year period, with my guides revealing to me after my third hospitalisation that my shamanic initiation was finally over and I was ready!

There's a saying in comedy that "It's all about the timing", and my guides have the edge-of-your-seat kind of timing that's left me saying, "Oh right, so that's what that was about. Yeah okay, I see what you did there".

So here she is, finally, the first book of three, a joint effort. And don't worry – I do already see the complete irony in all of this; that this book is about mental health, half-written by a bunch of my invisible friends and a group of extra-terrestrials. ET phone home! Let's go!

Hope you enjoy the ride!

Marie
ANT✤INETTE

Introduction

I am no stranger to depression, anxiety and suicidal thoughts, and I want you to know that I still experience these regularly to some degree. If I had told a doctor just last week the range of emotions I was wildly swinging between, I would have certainly been met with concern, a label and an offer to remedy the situation with a script for some kind of medication.

But I know doctors don't look after emotional health. It is purely physical. They are called 'general' practitioners after all, and most of the time they can only treat us 'generally speaking'. They are not mental health experts! The specialisation of mental health generally seems to lie in the hands of psychiatrists. However, psychiatrists are medically trained and 'indoctrinated' into using the *Diagnostic and Statistical Manual of Mental Disorders (DSM)*, with an array of pharmaceutical drugs to treat these ailments. It's interesting to note that the word 'indoctrinate' is defined by the Google dictionary as to "teach a person or group to accept a set of beliefs uncritically".

Have you ever researched for yourself the history of psychiatry? It's wise to question what we put our faith in, and these days a lot of us do; but for those who haven't, I've taken the liberty of including a brief insight. The word psychiatry comes from the words *psyche*, a Greek word meaning soul, and *iatros*, meaning doctor. Johann Christian Reil was the pioneer who came up with this medical-sounding name in 1808. His theory was that the mind, or 'life energy', causes spiritual confusion or decay. His theory sounds spiritual, but patients were treated as animals, often whipped, tortured and shackled into submission of 'proper' behaviour. Wilhelm Griesinger was a German neurologist and psychiatrist and was the first to claim that mental illnesses are brain diseases. His theory was that the soul is a function of the brain, but he himself admitted that this was just his theory, which he developed without any evidence.

The medical industry often doesn't look at causes, just treatment. And so, when I'm out of balance, I use what I know and what I teach others. I wanted to say in this introduction that I don't claim to be an expert in mental health, but that didn't sit right with me. I am an expert! I mean, who decides who is an expert? If you count the lived experience I have had, along with the study of human behaviour, spirit and soul and the years of research I have done, then yes, you could say I know my shit!

With my esoteric expertise, you could say I offer a multi-dimensional framework that I am applying to the subject of mental health. But this expertise came from an insane (pun intended) and relentless pursuit to understand myself. It has been and always will be that little voice within me that leads the way.

Deep down, I have never really accepted that a brain disease was to blame for all my emotional imbalances. Brain chemistry issues, for me, just didn't cut it. I'm glad it didn't. Turns out 'it' wasn't. With no evidence anywhere that mental illness is caused by a chemical imbalance, it's one of the biggest scams of the century! So rather than say I'm not an expert, I'd rather say I'm not perfect. It's easy to see the smiling image of me on this cover and say wow, she's happy, she's got it together. Looks can be deceiving. As I said, you should have seen me last week! My point is, I am not 'cured' of the myriad of mental health symptoms and I'm not 'happy' every day. I still have mood swings that would be concerning in the medical field.

I could take a tablet to feel better. When you have a headache, you take a Panadol, right? See? Right there is our conditioning to believe that pain needs to be eradicated rather than examined. It appears we have become a quick-fix, pleasure-seeking society that avoids discomfort at all costs.

And this extends to anything in society. Anything that doesn't look right or sound right is frowned upon. Anything that is DIFFERENT to what is normal. Norm-all! What does that even mean, anyway? I'm not Norm, I'm Marie. Why do I have to be a Norm with all the other Norms? It's the acceptance of my extreme sensitivities to energies – me being Marie and not some dude called Norm – that produces that happy smiling face you see on the front cover. A picture paints a thousand words, and that shining spirit that some of you may feel even through that picture is a result of me following my soul purpose!

Through my own self-development and spiritual journey, I discovered that as I healed within from my adverse childhood experiences, awakenings began to occur. Spontaneous esoteric experiences became frequent. I struggled to make sense of the synchronicities, psychic phenomena, dreams, visions and inner voices and callings, which were getting louder. The more I tried to silence them and just live a simple existence and try to fit in, the more depressed, anxious and ungrounded I became. I lost friends and felt the disapproval of family when I shared what I discovered, and most of the time I was treated with suspicion and fear. This made me retreat inwards for answers. The blessing in disguise was that I had no-one to help or understand me except spirit itself, and so my relationship with the divine grew!

I discovered shamanism around this time and searched for a physical teacher to assist me, but once again I was led back to the voice within. That voice informed me that there were two types of initiation. One was by having a physical teacher, and the other was to be initiated by spirit, the latter being the harder path. Well, ain't that the truth! I came to understand that I could enter altered states of consciousness at will and that I was not psychotic or insane, just a soul traveller who had to learn how to travel those worlds. When I learnt to embrace all my extrasensory capabilities through both physical and non-physical worlds, without fear of judgement, the more I shone and the more I could help people using my access to these worlds.

Following my path and the teachings so graciously afforded to me is what keeps me on an even keel. If something is amiss within me, I investigate and do my own diagnostics check to see what's happening with my little machine. My first port of call is to always see where it is within me that I'm not following my truth. I've learnt that vibrational alignment is important. If I'm not being authentic with myself and living what society or other people want me to be, then I'm going to be misfiring and not running on all cylinders.

I check for energetic and etheric causes such as entity attachments, in case I've picked up a hitchhiker from the spirit world somewhere along the line. I check for psychic attack and emotional attachments. I check to see if I am harbouring any unresolved anger or resentments or not allowing myself to feel sad over something that needs to be expressed. I know suppressed emotions are a killer (quite literally). I see where I can plan to sort things out with others. I choose these battles wisely. If I feel I may not be well received, I express these emotions through writing it out or through support from a friend.

I check to see if my physical needs are being met through physical exercise. Am I getting enough fresh air and time in nature, and am I challenging myself enough to receive a healthy amount of serotonin and endorphins? If I realise I'm not, I go and I go immediately. If I'm tired I drive to nature, but I go as if my life depends on it because often it does!

Am I getting enough nutrients in my system? If I eat shit, I feel shit. If I eat too much or not enough, I feel shit. I make adjustments, often cleaning out my body to give it a fresh start. When I have treated all these things and I'm *still* not right, I go and find Harry Potter. Kidding: I just ask my other imaginary friends!

My relentless searching, investigation and research have not only been fuelled by the need to understand myself, my family and the world at large; they have also been driven by all that I have learnt about the nature of addiction. After facing my addiction issues by ceasing all use of drugs and alcohol, I realised I could never return to them. And whenever I did, albeit temporarily, I learnt I was more sensitive than ever. This led me to foster an attitude and practise of looking within for answers. It was a life and death issue and I was somewhat forced into looking at alternative solutions. A blessing in disguise.

I realised that seeking a drug or any other addictive practice (including gambling, sex, food, shopping, work, etc.) was really about a lost soul blindly and desperately looking for solutions in all the wrong places, and this blind seeking only led to more problems.

It has taken a lot of courage for me to complete this book and speak in a manner of truth that sits well with me, because what my heart and soul wants to shout from the rooftops goes against most people's mainstream beliefs. They say it takes balls to stand out. I actually hate that saying! It insinuates that courage is a masculine thing. When describing something courageous, I like to say it takes wings (and not the Red Bull kind!)

What I want to shout out is that perhaps we've all been wildly and desperately searching in all the wrong places for ways to feel better, only perpetuating the problem further. In our attempts to feel better and quickly eradicate pain, have we fallen victim to the biggest drug suppliers in the world – Big Pharma?

Have we subconsciously allowed the medical field to fool us into believing we are seriously ill and need their medicines to balance us out? Relational therapies still seem to take a back seat in treatment options, despite ever-growing evidence of the brain's plasticity. Neuroscience studies are revealing that new neural pathways can be formed from relational-based counselling in the same way that medications appear to affect brain activity.

When looking at the side effects of mental health medications, it starts to become very concerning. Are the risks worth it? Side effects include disruption and impairment of normal brain function, drug-induced chemical imbalance in the brain, dystonia, fatigue, twitching, sedation, memory loss, concentration difficulties, headaches and, the most ironic of all, suicidal thoughts and tendencies. There are obviously cases where pharmaceutical remedy is needed to bring a person back into this reality safely, or where a person is feeling unsafe and poses a risk to themselves or others, but often the real causes are overlooked and dependence is formed.

In my research over the years and for this book, I have found many other professionals who have questioned the status quo and, rather speak of their work here, I've included their books in my recommended reading list at the back. I have decided that you can do further reading of your own to better assist you if you feel inclined. A lot of authors in their introductions explain how to read their book. I don't care how you read this one, but I've tried to write it in a way that makes it hard to put down!

In this book, you will find information, tools and stories that shed light on other contributing factors of a spiritual and soul nature, which look like mental health symptoms on the surface but can be viewed as signs and signals of awakening, transformation and soul emergence. This book is dedicated to tools that can assist you on your journey from a soul perspective. You will find that there is some repetition in different ways throughout the keys. This has been deliberate and I was guided to leave the repetition, as repetition is a basis for learning. Think of it like a multi-faceted diamond, if you will.

In addition, I have not attempted to cover every single diagnosis that appears in the DSM because this book would be too long. (A bit like the manual itself!) Instead, I have mentioned the main ones for which I can offer a soul approach.

I believe the 'mentally ill' or 'mentally disordered' people in our world are the most misunderstood beings on the planet. Our health system has been trying to treat a spiritual and soul issue with physical, biological remedy and, let's face it, for a lot of people out there, it's simply not working. These amazing, sensitive and often spiritually aware, psychic, advanced beings are being drugged, segregated, ostracised, and numbed down by a system that does not support holistic healing, understanding or full recovery.

It's interesting to note that when you split the word diagnosis, you get die-gnosis. *Gnosis* means 'knowledge of spiritual mysteries'. It's well known that the world's major spiritual teachings and wisdom have been kept hidden in secret societies and are not well understood by the mainstream population. But times are changing! It is my hope that the contents of this book refresh your spirit and liberate your soul.

While there has been no shortage of alleged biochemical explanations for psychiatric conditions ... not one has been proven. Quite the contrary. In every instance where such an imbalance was thought to have been found, it was later proven false.

DR JOSEPH GLENMULLEN, HARVARD MEDICAL SCHOOL PSYCHIATRIST

The way things get into the DSM is not based on blood test or brain scan or physical findings. It's based on descriptions of behaviour. And that's what the whole psychiatry system is.

DR COLIN ROSS, PSYCHIATRIST

Virtually anyone at any given time can meet the criteria for bipolar disorder or ADHD. Anyone. And the problem is everyone diagnosed with even one of these 'illnesses' triggers the pill dispenser.

DR STEFAN KRUSZEWSKI, PSYCHIATRIST

Despite more than two hundred years of intensive research, no commonly diagnosed psychiatric disorders have proven to be either genetic or biological in origin, including schizophrenia, major depression, manic-depressive disorder, the various anxiety disorders, and childhood disorders such as attention-deficit hyperactivity. At present there are no known biochemical imbalances in the brain of typical psychiatric patients – until they are given psychiatric drugs.

PETER BREGGIN, PSYCHIATRIST

No behaviour or misbehaviour is a disease or can be a disease. That's not what diseases are. Diseases are malfunctions of the human body, of the heart, the liver, the kidney, the brain. Typhoid fever is a disease. Spring fever is not a disease; it is a figure of speech, a metaphoric disease. All mental diseases are metaphoric diseases, misrepresented as real diseases and mistaken for real diseases.

THOMAS SZASZ, PROFESSOR OF PSYCHIATRY

The 12 Keys

The Key of Acceptance

If you begin to understand what you are without trying to change it, then what you are undergoes a transformation.

Jiddu Krishnamurti

Many years ago I was sitting with a friend of mine at a cafe. As we began talking, I saw an expression of pain on his face, with his forehead all wrinkled up. When I asked him what was wrong, he told me that he had a migraine. In that moment, because I cared for my friend, I thought in my head, "I wish he didn't have this migraine, what a poor thing". And then suddenly I could feel my forehead crease up with my head starting to throb. I looked up at my friend half-smiling at me, saying "Give it back. It's not yours to take". I was fascinated that he was so calmly asking for it back and he had full awareness of what had just happened.

Confused, I said to him, "I'm not even sure how I've taken it; I don't know how to give it back". Smiling, he said, "Just send it back", as if it were obvious. Not wanting my friend to be in pain, but knowing it wasn't mine, I sent the headache back with my mental intention. I really didn't think it was going to work, but I could see the moment it arrived back in his body by the strain that reappeared on his face. It was a valuable lesson for me about how easily we can unconsciously

1

take on other people's issues. Coincidentally it was also a bonus because with his headache back, he didn't feel like eating his cake!

Super Sensitives

The mental health system seeks to conform all of us into one standard of being. The reality is that we all think differently and we also all *feel* differently. Some of us don't feel at all because we have become numb in some way, while some feel so deeply that it feels like their heart is literally shattering into a million pieces. If you fall into the deeper and more sensitive category, you're more likely to experience depression, anxiety and mood swings as you swing wildly from emotions that, most of the time, you don't understand. I totally relate; I'm a swinger too! It's important to understand that you may fall into a different category to most when it comes to handling emotions, which can better serve you to see that you are not disordered, just different.

Highly sensitive people, or super sensitives, are more sensitive than most to all energies. Because of this sensitivity and the fact that emotions are also energy, crowded places and toxic environments where there is a lot of anger and frustration easily overwhelm a sensitive. Dr Elaine Aron, the originator of the term 'highly sensitive person', defines it this way:

> **A Highly Sensitive Person (HSP) has a sensitive nervous system, is aware of subtleties in his/her surroundings, and is more easily overwhelmed when in a highly stimulating environment.**

HSPs may also be sensitive to larger field energies. Then there are those that are extra-super sensitive, who feel the vibration and frequency and emotions of not only their local communities, but the world at large and even the earth system. I once worked with a client in my counselling practice who came to me because she was severely depressed. When we unpacked what her depression was about, it was her deep empathic nature contributing to her sensitivity to the world at large. She was sad because of the violence, she was sad because of the wars, she was sad because people didn't get along with one another and she was heavily impacted by these energies.

Super sensitives may also be sensitive to stimulants such as coffee, sugar and preservatives, which can cause things like hyperactivity and inability to concentrate, which bring in such labels as Attention Deficit Disorder (ADD) and Attention Deficit Hyperactivity Disorder (ADHD). HSPs can also be empaths, but not all HSPs are empaths as well.

For the sensitive souls who unknowingly have access to the non-physical realms and dimensions, life is extremely hard. You don't seem to fit into the ordinary, but rather find yourself in the extraordinary realm. You may find yourself outcast, labelled with titles such as crazy, weird, nuts, bonkers, mad – the list goes on; you get the idea.

You feel inextricably different, yet you don't exactly know why. You feel things and have reactions that people don't understand. You may avoid people and things and then be over-the-top. You have thoughts, feelings and experiences that you keep to yourself because sharing them may confirm that you are indeed mad.

You see synchronicities all the time and somehow know that there is a grand design working in perfect harmony, yet you can't seem to find that harmony in yourself. You are deeply impacted by the violence perpetuated by humans against each other and towards animals and nature. You see other people's disdain towards you and sometimes wish you were different. You try to fit in, try to be normal, wondering what the hell it is that's wrong with you. Deep inside you may feel like you are harbouring a secret, but you don't even know what that secret is. You feel like an alien, sometimes to your own family. You don't know why you feel this way, but you feel it.

Empaths

Empaths literally feel everything. They have the ability to scan a room and feel the vibe emanating from everyone in it. They can always tell when something is wrong. They don't know how they know it, they just do. They pick up on the subtle emotions or energies. They are easily moved by art and equally horrified by acts of violence. Even though they can be social, they secretly prefer to do things solo. They have powerful imaginations and their intuition is high.

If you're an empath, loud and noisy places may irritate you. You feel other people's emotions as if they were your own and this is where you can get stuck in people-pleasing. You naturally have a difficulty with saying no. You feel things deeply and cry easily. You may be regarded as eccentric.

Empaths have a bullshit radar that's so finely tuned that lying to them is impossible and they can know what you're feeling, even if you don't! Empaths feel the emotion someone is trying to hide behind a fake smile. If you try and tell an empath that you're not angry when you are, they will react to the emotion and therefore be hurt by the lie. This is because they feel the unseen energy and know the agenda of someone who is trying to manipulate or fool them. Interpersonal relationships are extremely hard for sensitive types because they are often absorbing and reacting to the other person's emotions and feelings. This can be highly confusing. And because of the bullshit radar, empaths need people who aren't fake and have the kind of rigorous honesty usually found in someone with Asperger's! When empaths ask, 'Does my bum look big in this?'

they need the 'Yes it does honey, the other outfit was more flattering on you' kind of honesty.

Because empaths naturally take on other people's emotions as their own, they often feel overwhelmed and can develop chronic lethargy along with depression and anxiety. Empaths are often labelled with bipolar disorder or even borderline personality disorder because of their erratic and swinging emotions, but it's usually caused by carrying other people's emotions around like heavy baggage. Learning healthy boundaries is key for empaths. You are only responsible for your own emotions, and being responsible for other people is actually hurting, not helping. Responsibility is the ability to respond, and if you are taking on other people's feelings, you are ripping them off, depriving them of being able to respond to their own issue. If you see it as disempowering and harmful, then you may be more inclined to let go of this behaviour.

This, of course, is difficult when dealing with people who behave as if they cannot respond and they are sinking in quicksand. They are stuck in victimhood, and I call them the quicksand people because no matter what solutions you offer, they seem to have an intense victim energy and be stuck in self-pity. You may find this very draining, as though the life force is being sucked out of you. It's regarded as 'learned helplessness', a theory developed by Martin Seligman. Learned helplessness often originates from a history of painful experiences where there was no escape, and is also often passed down from a helpless parent who won't ever take responsibility for how they feel.

The balance of self-care and letting go of others is a challenge for empaths. For an empath, a good question to ask regularly when you're overwhelmed about an emotion is, "Is this mine or someone else's?" If it feels like someone else's, you can literally shake it off your body by mentally imagining it leaving you as you stroke it off your arms and torso with your hands. You can send it into Mother Earth or Father Sky or to the creator of all that is for transmutation.

Regular grounding exercises, keeping things simple, extra breaks and naps and honouring your own emotions will all help to bring you equilibrium. Sensitives and empaths who accept their sensitivity can lower the risk of mental health symptoms by avoiding caffeine and sugar, getting adequate sleep and spending more time in nature. A daily energy protection is highly recommended to assist you to stay within your own emotional vibration field. This is easier said than done for empaths, but practice makes perfect. Knowing full well that this is a very important thing to keep you at an even state is also going to help inspire you to keep up this way of living.

If you have identified that what you are carrying is actually yours, it's important to note that from a soul perspective, there are no good or bad feelings. The Zen ideology says, "It just is". There are many teachings by different authors from various cultures who have spoken about this. How often do you live it? We are led to believe that if we are not happy, something is wrong. If we're not happy, it makes other people uncomfortable. If we're not happy, people want to change it.

Healthy inquiry without judgement of your emotions will help you to uncover what your inner self needs. Your emotions can be used as your internal GPS to help you navigate your way through life. Because all feelings and emotions are energy in motion, they need to move and flow through the body. A lot of illness occurs because of stuck emotions.

Taking on Illness

Empaths are often past-life healers and shamans who know how to transmute illness by drawing the sickness into their own body and then releasing it to light. Often, they are the accidental heroes who are intuitively taking on other people's emotions and illnesses, forgetting the important part of clearing it from their own bodies.

These natural healers who are not aware of how energy works may find themselves suddenly sick. Left unchecked over time, they may also be diagnosed with a mental illness based on these unexplainable symptoms which, in truth, don't even belong to them. When we look at things from a deeper level, we start to see the clarity of what may really be going on.

Think about the headache I took from my friend. Had he not been spiritually insightful enough to explain what had happened, I would have walked away from that lunch date with a migraine and no extra cake!

I will give you another example of the power of taking on another person's emotions. It's a true story about what happened with my mother when I was a wannabe healer over 15 years ago. I'd only done a very short energy healing course, more out of curiosity than anything. I was much younger and much more inexperienced. I had a strong longing to heal my mother, who was often pleading for help in her traumatic learned-helplessness state. I asked her if she would like me to do a healing, so I did.

I remember excitedly telling my brother over the phone what I was about to do. He warned me, saying, "You have to be careful with whatever you're pulling out of Mum and where that goes". With more than a hint of stubborn arrogance I told him I knew what I was doing. As I began to practise what I had learnt only the day before, I was both fascinated and surprised at what occurred next. Her body began to convulse and shake as she let out an array of noises and screams loud enough to make the neighbours think some hideous crime was unfolding. I wondered if we would end up with police knocking on the door, but I stayed calm as she continued to release things in a way that resembled an exorcism. Every chakra point I worked on seemed to hold great pain and energy blockages as I saw them being released. As I worked on her throat, for example, she would start to cough, and when I worked on her heart she would sob. It looked like it was going very well. When I finished, she appeared exhausted but calm, smiling at me and saying, "It's all gone, it's all gone, thank you".

But what happened to me after this healing was quite intense. For the next 12 months she reportedly had a marked change, but I experienced a very dark and deep depression. I began to have flashes of myself locked in some sort of dark room with no escape, with just a little window. I had no motivation for anything in my life. There were times that I couldn't go to college or attend my own therapy sessions.

On an intuitive level, I knew that what was happening to me wasn't mine. I somehow knew that the memory flashes were not my own. There were times I nearly went on medication because I just didn't know what else to do. I was eventually able to recover when I saw a psychic for a tarot reading and she turned out to be a shamanic healer. The moment I walked in, she looked at me sternly and said, "You, my dear, must learn the lesson that you must heal yourself before you attempt to heal your mother". She helped to clear what I had taken on.

The question is there to be asked. With some people who are suffering major bouts of depression and anxiety, is it their emotions that they're carrying or somebody else's? Is it that they are depressed? Or are they just overwhelmed by everyone else's baggage? Are they bipolar or borderline or just the wounded healer masquerading as an empath? Same same but different.

The Clairs

I have described the four types of psychic ability so that you can understand them, so that if you experience them, you have a point of reference. I used to see many clients in my counselling practice that would describe these experiences as strange, who had become anxious and ungrounded. What they were experiencing was prefaced with, "This is going to sound crazy ...", or "You're going to think I'm mad, but ..."

As you move along your spiritual journey, more and more experiences tend to show up because as you awaken, so too do your extraordinary senses. You are not crazy, nor gifted; these abilities are your divine birthright.

Clairvoyance: This is the more widely known ability. This is a psychic 'seeing' ability where images, scenes or information are shown or seen with the third eye. These images or scenes can come through dreaming or meditative states or, if well developed, can come at any time in an awakened state through the mind. The images or scenes can be from the future, about a person, from a past life, etc. They may be confusing if they come randomly to someone but they all have meaning and relevance.

Clairaudience: This is a psychic 'hearing' ability. This is through an 'inner' hearing which is like receiving information telepathically. Telepathy is communication through the form of thought. Some people do not realise that they have this skill or ability because they do not differentiate their own thought from a thought that may come in from another source. This is because they are expecting to hear an outer voice. Clairaudience can be developed by practising regular mindfulness through meditative practice and developing what is known as the 'observer' so that the inner hearing can be more recognised. Empaths sometimes have the ability to hear other people's thoughts and can hear guidance through an audible outer voice.

Clairsentience: This is a psychic 'feeling' ability, often referred to as a 'gut' or intuitive feeling. A gut feeling is best described as having a good, bad or indifferent feeling towards something without any other information to provide evidence for that feeling. For example, you may feel extremely uncomfortable and frightened in a place and not know why, only to find out that a violent crime happened there. You may receive information through feelings or bodily sensations. A very common bodily sensation is hairs standing on end or goose bumps. Some people have related this to fear from conditioning through horror movies, but this sensation is a signal for truth.

Claircognizance: This refers to an inner knowing without any conceivable doubt that something is true. Claircognizance is an interesting ability to have and use, especially on its own without the other abilities, as it simply feels like the information gained has come out of nowhere at no time – it is just known! It is a skill based on ESP (extrasensory perception), also called the sixth sense, which includes reception of information not gained through the recognised physical senses but sensed with the mind. This is the hardest sense to develop and grow as it relies heavily on trust and faith and noting of experience to develop. It's often confusing because thoughts, ideas and guidance just pop into your head and appear to download out of nowhere. It may be disconcerting to realise that you know things ahead of time or know about a particular place or subject without having researched it.

You may at times know how sensitive you are and wish it was not the case. Wishing yourself to be different and be like everyone else will not help you and is the difference between feeling like you are cursed or gifted. Mental and emotional equilibrium will only come when you embrace yourself as you. In all great teachings of loving yourself, this is the truth that will help liberate you. If you're highly sensitive, an empath or finding yourself having some weird out-of-this-world experience, embrace it, seek to understand it and it will no longer be something you wish you weren't. Highly sensitive people who honour their difference, learn healthy boundaries, and work on staying out of co-dependant behaviours can really thrive! When accepted, embraced and understood, HSPs and empaths actually have a great set of extraordinary skills that help them to excel as artists, writers, actors, healers and psychics. Although it's a challenge to be sensitive in a harsh world, the set of character traits can be viewed as a hindrance or blessing. Same same but different.

Here are the Pleiadians on acceptance, offering their planetary view.

The Pleiadians on Acceptance

There are those of you who are different and have been pre-programmed by yourselves as souls to be different. You have chosen to enter this experience with specific energy centres already open. Namely, your crown chakras, to remind you of your existence before you came into form. You have also chosen to have your heart energy centres a little more open. This means you have allowed these centres to be open as you came into form rather than from just this lifetime. Therefore, it feels like you were born with your heart on your sleeve. This is why you are so sensitive to energies and especially those that oppose unconditional love. Any form of cruelty makes your insides shudder. Harsh words and sounds hurt your minds and hearts. You feel deeply and resonate with beauty. You want to love and help your fellow man. You seek peace and harmony. These all sound so gracious. But gracious they are not to a selfish, cold, unemotional world. You sensitives do not fit into harsh, noisy and brash environments and trying to will only cause distress.

You feel uncomfortable in social situations and some of you have learnt to mask this deep sensitivity well. Sensitivity is not welcome in most arenas. You are like a sponge for energy as your soul knows how to transmute such energies in a flash. You have had an experience at one time or other in another time and existence of being able to blast your way through denser energies, converting them to light as you go. You have chosen to anchor these energies into the earth grids, for a harsh world needs some alternate energy. Do you see? Do you see that just by being you, you are assisting to balance the energies here? These very words may help you remember. Remember the choice you made. This is why sometimes you have felt so alien to this existence. Different to your peers, to your families.

Rather than trying to suppress it or change it or wish it were different, embrace it, and accept it. See it as your asset, your ally. It serves those around you. It's what assists you to be creative, to see things in a different light, to be able to assist another through your very presence. Your empathy for others helps them feel not so alone. Your care and concern holds a great degree of unconditional love; however, you sensitives need a special kind of care. A special kind of lesson in this world. And that lesson is unconditional love for the self. To love yourselves no matter what. To balance the care and concern you feel for others and your environment with the care and concern for yourself. For you are your best asset in this world. Self-preservation is key if you are to be of assistance. It is imperative that you learn that putting yourself first is not selfish, but indeed the opposite. That you must treat yourself as an asset. That your big wide-open heart is an asset, not a curse, when used wisely. It is meant to be used as an energetic field and as an example, not to pull anyone else out of their own misery. Empathy states that we are in this together, not 'I'll feel this for you so that you don't have to'. You are all-powerful creators, and just because you emit rays of unconditional love does not mean that the next person cannot also do that. Each soul has its lesson.

Accept your ability to sense, know, feel and hear the non-physical. Use it to guide you. To show and light your way rather than be afraid by it, or rather the opposite, where you may be excited by it but miss the opportunity it presents to you. The opportunity of wise creation. For without the sensitives here on this planet, without the empaths, the earth herself has no empathic witness to see, feel and understand that she is being harmed and destroyed. Through the lens of your empathic souls, you return harmony to the whole. Allow yourself to feel, let it out, do not stifle it, soothe yourself as your expressions arise and accept the difference that you are making in this world by being you.

Armed with the Key of Acceptance, it's time to obtain the Key of Awareness.

The Key of Awareness

**Full awareness requires you to go beyond using
not only two eyes, but three; there you will find
a full reality of what there is to see.**

Me

Non-physical Entities

Let me introduce you to a young 10-year-old called Paul, who is on the autism spectrum. His mother knew of my work and called, asking for a session. She told me that he had become very confused, not wanting to eat and not wanting to sleep. Paul had described to her that someone he called 'Bossy Worry' was giving him directions for what to do, and she had seen him whispering to someone as he tried to sleep.

Interestingly, the symptoms of not eating and sleeping are common to those who have bipolar disorder, and they are the warning signs of going into a manic and psychotic episode. His mother was open-minded enough to realise it could be an entity attachment.

So, I facilitated a session with her and chose to have Paul present so he too could be involved and learn from this experience. When I tuned into his energy I could see that Bossy Worry was another boy similar to his age who was a stuck spirit. He had died in a fire in the house that stood there before the current one was built. Not knowing he was dead, he was a wandering spirit who had attached to Paul because of his open energy fields. I could see that the boy didn't understand why he couldn't eat and sleep like his newfound friend, who seemed to be able to sense him. He had been 'worried and bossy' by saying to Paul that if he couldn't eat and sleep, neither should he!

I called in this lost boy's guides and ancestors to cross him over. When he realised what was going on, he was very apologetic for being so bossy! He was grateful that he would be going home, saying he didn't feel trapped anymore. He crossed the bridge of light and said there would be no more Bossy Worry around anymore for Paul, with a big smile on his face. Paul cheered in delight and said, happy and relieved, "Goodbye, Bossy Worry", as I told him the boy was crossing the bridge into the light.

Interestingly, Paul's grandfather on the father's side was at the entry to the bridge of light wanting to get a message through to Paul. He instructed me not to edit the message in any way, perhaps sensing my inclination to believe that Paul may not understand. So I told Paul everything. His grandfather wanted him to know that Paul was a light worker, one of many, and that when he was an adult he would be helping many people just like him. He wanted him to know that how he was should be seen as a blessing and not a burden. He said that Paul had chosen to have this condition so that he could help others when he was older with the same condition. He said that he was going to help many boys and men like him.

Grandfather also had a message for his mother and father, and said it would be best that they stopped viewing their son as someone with a condition or limitation and that their energy of limitation towards him could affect him. He wanted to remind them that it was Paul's choice as a soul to have this experience. He went on to say that they needed to stop trying to make him conform to society's expectations; that his rawness and direct honesty was a gift in this world and opposite of the normalcy in society to lie, be polite and nice to appease others. He completed his message by saying that Paul, through his experience, would be paving a new way forward in the world of living in truth and integrity, being a way-shower to others in the world.

The Other Side of the Veil

Ghosts and demons are the most common things people have been conditioned to understand about the afterlife from movies and TV shows. As a society, we have been subliminally brainwashed to live in fear when it comes to death. There are some cultures that celebrate death and contain advanced knowledge about the afterlife, such as indigenous cultures and the ancient Egyptians. Have you ever noticed there aren't as many shows about angels, ascended masters or good galactic dudes out there? No wonder so many people fear investigating the paranormal or the unknown of what's on the other side.

What isn't widely known, or is grossly misunderstood, is the ability for those who are 'dead' to affect the living. I use inverted commas here because they are not really dead, just in another form. They have the ability to affect us energetically, both constructively and destructively. How they will affect us depends on exactly 'where' they are – whether they are in the light, meaning ascended into the heavenly state (state meaning a state of consciousness and not a place), or stuck to the earth's field of consciousness.

With all the conditioning, it's easy to get all "Oh shit, we need an exorcism now, we'd better crack out the garlic or salt". There might be religious beliefs that involve the devil, but in the hundreds of cases I've come across with denser energies who have no intention of crossing over to the light, I have learnt that there really is nothing to fear. Everything comes from source and will return to the light eventually.

I've often felt like a sister out of the TV series *Charmed* because of some of the things I've seen. There is all manner of beings including dark lords and demons that make *Star Wars* and *Men in Black* feel very real! You could say that the good/bad, light/dark armies extend out across all the soul planes inter-dimensionally and intra-dimensionally, and many also have a job to do regarding fear. They are often mirroring back our own negative beliefs on this level. From a soul perspective, how can you learn to overcome fear when fear isn't present?

Compassion is warranted as these beings are suffering soul amnesia like the rest of us, and those in the dark really believe they are working for humanity's good, just from a very warped perspective. I teach a lot about the 'dark side of the light' through my workshops because it is misunderstood, even by those working as psychics and healers in the spiritual arenas. The most important thing to know is that they feed off fear, so staying out of the vibration of fear and in an energy of love is your best protection. Think of the lower vibrational energies being on one radio station frequency and higher vibes such as love and forgiveness on another. These entities cannot tune into your radio station if you are in love. It's a different frequency and they can't even connect to you because you're on a different wavelength!

Positive Effects

If you knew who walked beside you at all times, on the path that you have chosen, you could never experience fear or doubt again.

Wayne W. Dyer

Beings who have passed on in their journey and reached the light understand the truth of our reality on this earth. They have complete understanding of their soul's journey and why they had their existence on this plane. To top it off, they can see everything that is going on and provide assistance to the living. In my practice I have found that, usually, grandmothers or grandfathers are assigned as guardians to their granddaughters and grandsons. They are able to give valuable insight into the person's life and guide them on their path here. How I ascertain whether a spirit is in the light or not is usually by the way they look and how I feel. Because everything is made up of energy and the spirit beings are vibrating at an energetic level, I understand that if I feel fear or apprehension, then they are certainly not in the light. Those who have already crossed over into the light emanate an unbelievable sense of joy, love, freedom and wisdom as I communicate with them. I'm able to feel every part of their being and every part of the way they wish to communicate. It is an amazing experience and I feel very blessed to be able to do this work. It has brought so much joy and peace to the people that I offer messages to.

Interaction with the other side, with spirits who are in the heavenly state and not what we call earthbound, can help to improve our emotional and mental state in ways beyond what any medication or therapy can do. It's one of the reasons I work predominately from a healing framework now, although I have been trained in psychotherapy. It can take months in therapy to heal what can be healed on the inner planes in one session. Contact with loved ones who have passed over can bring great love, insight and healing.

The Sceptic

I once had a big Maori man come and see me when I was working as a psychic reader in a store. I don't actually remember his name, so let's just call him 'the sceptic'. He walked in and told me straight off the bat that he didn't really want a reading, but his friend was having one next door. He said he didn't believe in all this mumbo-jumbo but his friend had paid for it and insisted he have one too. He assured me it was okay if we just sat and chatted for the half hour. I was fine with that until I felt his father's presence in the room, who informed me with great urgency that he had something to say to his son!

I told him I didn't mind what he believed, but that his father was standing beside me and wanted to speak to him. "Are you open to hearing what he has to say?" I asked. The man was instantly shocked and took a moment before agreeing to listen. I passed on that his father was distressed that he was following in the same footsteps as him. He apologised for not being a good father to him while he was alive, describing himself as a violent alcoholic. He said he had abandoned him and his brother when his relationship with their mother failed. He spoke about the man's recent separation from his partner and the fact that he had not seen his own two boys and urged him not to abandon them as he had done with him.

The man was in shock, with tears rolling down his face as I told him all of this. He began to sob deeply. He confessed that he had not cried in 10 years. I passed on that his father was deeply, deeply sorry for not being the father that he could have been to him and was now trying to make amends to him from the other side. He asked his son to forgive him and through his tears, the man accepted, saying thank you to his father and to me.

I mentioned earlier the size and nationality of this man, because in our society it's often not acceptable for a man to cry and show his emotions. This particular reading for this gentleman was incredibly healing, and he walked out not only a believer but told me he was determined not to repeat the generational pattern of abandonment. He then bowled his mate over with a big hug, thanking him for shouting him a reading. I believe it is everyone's divine right to have access to and knowledge of the non-physical realms so that they can use the all-loving, all-encompassing light, truth and knowledge that can assist us in our everyday lives to create a life beyond our wildest dreams!

Negative Effects

Earthbound spirits, often referred to as ghosts, can affect a person's mental health without the conscious awareness of the person. When a person dies, the only thing that really changes is that their body ceases to exist. The person's consciousness remains, so their spirit then leaves the body and is free to travel back home to 'light' or 'heaven' or 'source'. If the person has died, suddenly or tragically, their consciousness remains in shock, and just as they were 'in body', they may go into shock caused by the trauma, and not actually witness their own death due to a block in memory or denial.

This shock prevents them from knowing that they have died and they will still see, hear and sense the world as they knew it. The best way to understand these phenomena is via the portrayal of an earthbound spirit in the movie *The Sixth Sense*, starring Bruce Willis. This movie is the best portrayal of an earthbound spirit that I have ever seen. Other people, after their bodies cease to exist, may become aware of the light or be drawn to it, but stay to try and complete 'unfinished business', while others do not see or get drawn to the light because their vibration or frequency is not attuned to the light. Religious views may have people believing that they must earn their space in heaven with a certain number of good deeds in their life, but reaching the light is actually quite scientific. Light is as much a density as it is a frequency.

In the ancient Egyptian book of the dead, there is a description of the Goddess called Maat (whom I know well, as you will discover later on in the book) who was said to be the judge of such vibration.

It was said that she would weigh one's heart (conscience) against the feather of truth and justice (known as the feather of Maat). If the heart was as light as a feather and nearly weightless, this indicated that the deceased soul was not burdened with sin and evil (really just words for density) and could pass to the heavenly realms.

When something is light, it weighs less. The opposite of light is heavy. Emotions such as hate, greed, envy, jealousy and resentment are heavy in density. If a person has a lot of these thoughts, emotions or unfinished business in their consciousness, they cannot rise to the light. They can have these feelings transformed by an experience that can lift these, either by spirit beings, who can be passed-over ancestors who come and make themselves known to the spirit to try and guide them to the light, or by a psychic medium in the 3D world they just left who can see, hear, and feel them and guide them to the light. This is known as crossing a spirit over into the light. The TV show *The Ghost Whisperer* depicts this well in its many episodes of 'stuck' spirits. Those with unfinished business or confused spirits are known as ghosts, who cause hauntings and possessions and can interfere on the earthly realms although they are not in body.

I have seen this play out many times when I have assisted spirits to cross over, often having to counsel them to help them release fear and resentment. I once moved on a spirit who had killed himself in the family home. After ten years, he believed he was still 'living' in the house, full of anger and rage and very pissed off that his brother had taken over his room! It took me a few hours where I facilitated a dialogue been the physical and non-physical brother so he could come to a place of peace. When he finally did, it was beautiful. A big amazing white sparkling light filled a corner of the room along with some of his spiritual guides who were there to help him transition, and into the light he stepped and disappeared.

Other ways in which an earthbound entity can affect someone can be:

◊   Feeling like energy is constantly drained (life force energy)

◊   Undeniable and unexplainable feelings of anger or despair

◊   Not feeling like you are you, but you can't explain why

◊   Engaging in reckless and unusual non-typical behaviour

◊   Feeling irritable and somewhat aggressive with no apparent cause

◊   Having difficulty with friends and family with sudden disturbances in the relationship, without knowing why

◊   Hearing or sensing destructive ideas to harm self or others.

The list above is not an exhaustive one and, as you can see, it already looks like the symptoms of someone experiencing depression or another mental illness. Same same but different. There are also different types of unseen energies and ways in which they can affect you.

Attachment – Think of a parasite that attaches itself to a host who is unaware of it being there, and this will give you some idea. This is where an earthbound spirit attaches and feeds off energy over a period of time. Most of these that I have come across are simply lost spirits who don't know where else to go, who are often trying to be helpful to the living. There are earthbound spirits who are often roaming around, unaware they are actually dead, so when someone pleads for help to 'anyone', these spirits can come to this open invitation and become attached. For those of you wondering, I'll cover the other ways in which attachment happens in the Key of Vibration.

Tricksters – There are some spirits who know of the light and do not wish to cross over. They seem to *play* on the other side of the veil to wreak havoc. They have the ability to communicate both audibly and through mental telepathy. They often pose as ascended masters or other beings and can sometimes be referred to as false light beings. When working with any being that is communicating with you, it is always important to check whether they have your best interests at heart by asking them. There are also accidental tricksters, where a person may die with a lot of ego and has been a light worker in this life, but for some reason does not know that they have died. In their sense of importance, they believe they are helping people when they haven't even made their way to the light. They can also appear as the messiah, or an ascended master appearing to help you, but with ulterior motives.

Possession – This is when a spirit can enter inside and take control of the mind and decisions of a person, altering their personality completely. These spirits are either misguided or have a darker agenda and may know they are dead with no intention of wanting to go to the light. In religious texts, exorcisms are reported to solve these cases, but in my experience they rarely do, because the process of an exorcism is to send these entities back to hell. But that's not where they came from. They are beings of light who have forgotten who they are and are not essentially evil, just confused. Everything originates from source light. Sometimes earthbounds may do this out of desperation. I've had the Whoopi Goldberg experience from the movie *Ghost*, where a pushy spirit had jumped into my body to feel and see their loved one through me. I had to tell them to mind their manners and ask permission first.

Hauntings – This occurs when earthbound spirits attach themselves to a house, believing that it is still theirs and that the new occupants need to be moved on. In one of my house clearing cases I saw a vision of the lady who owned the house being kicked by a spirit, falling over and hurting her ankle. When I asked about this, she said she had indeed sprained her ankle in that place and felt like someone had pushed her, but thought she might have been mad to even think such a thing. When I connected with the spirit, it was a woman who believed that it was *her* house and was upset that this stranger was invading *her* space! The homeowner also reported noises, cigar smoke and perfume wafting from the lounge room at night. I told her not to worry as we would clear everything out. She seemed relieved and mentioned that one night when she couldn't sleep, she had sarcastically yelled out of frustration, "I'm not scared of you. If you want to party in my lounge room, well then you're welcome". As I entered her lounge area, I saw several spirits hanging out, drinking and smoking as if it were a bar! I had to explain to her that her invitation had been heard and there was indeed a party happening in her lounge room!

Psychic attack/curses – This is where people send ill intention, known as the evil eye in many European cultures. The intent of wishing someone harm can be unconscious or conscious and can be sent to a person, their life, or their family. Harm can affect the emotional, physical, spiritual, or mental state of a person. Those negative energies are typically projected in the form of thought, based on jealousy, envy, anger, or rage. A conscious attack can be compared to black magic and is often perpetuated from jealousy – for example, the victim's life is progressing forward while the attacker's is stagnant, and the attacker is often desperate and trying to get even and living in fear. It is important to note that when negative energy is consciously sent to someone with the intention of inflicting harm, what is sent is exactly what will be attracted upon the sender in their own life. The universal law of karma states that for every action there is a reaction.

Some of the symptoms of a psychic attack are: nightmares, fatigue, feeling aches and pains often in the same place, weakness, nausea, severe headaches accompanied by vomiting or dizziness, feeling paranoid like someone is out to get you, and feeling anxious and jumpy for no reason. Severe psychic attacks can render a person extremely mentally unstable and mimic mental health symptoms. I have experienced and seen these symptoms in some of my clients. It's more common than most people realise. Because I am able to see energy, I have literally been able to trace it back to the source of the person sending the intention. Sometimes it's a surprise to the person, but more often than not, the victim is aware of how the other person may feel. I have always taught that forgiveness is the key, never sending anything back but allowing it to be transmuted by unconditional love and light protection. Their own karma is really enough and, more than anything, these people need light and love in their lives.

It is important to note that sending love and light to someone is not really constructive; the highest blessing you can give someone is grace. When you send love and light, you could be harming them because their understanding of love may subconsciously equal pain, and there are many false *light* beings. It's important to send only unconditional love and *unconditional* light, and in this way you are actually affording the receiver grace.

The Pleiadians on Awareness

What is awareness, really? The full gamut of awareness is only a portion of what humanity currently holds in its hand. But times are changing and the scales, yes, they are tipping. They are tipping to more truth, to more light and to more awareness. There is much talk about protection in the spiritual arenas. It has been spoken of in many ancient cultures as the 'evil eye'. Protection has also been used to help with the invisible ones, the ones that normally go undetected. Now, if these worlds are real, these invisible realms where all this paranormal activity is going on, then why is their knowledge hidden, the knowledge used to create fear and 'horror' movies when in reality it is just the truth of a soul's journey?

Is there power in these fields that could be harnessed to work against humanity? Could these lower vibrational beings be tricked themselves into working for some false evil god to wreak havoc for the living from the other side? Perhaps there is an army of dark beings that the physical world is unaware of. We don't speak of this to create fear. Fear is the tool of those who wish to keep you unaware. To assist you, we shall speak about the law of the trinity. This law is the governing force behind the law of free will. You see, there are many laws that rule not only your universe but the cosmos. The law of attraction has come into your awareness and is known by many, but it is time for all laws to fully emerge and be understood so that everyone can have equal footing in the game of existence and the laws that govern creation can become equal once and for all.

Death is an illusion and this itself creates the real delusion. You are eternal beings who are travelling. Your ancients know that you are merely visitors to this place and they also know of the keys we speak of. For it is within their hearts that these keys reside. You are all ancients who hold these keys. You may know the saying, 'To lock someone up and throw away the key'? Well, we tell you this; some of you have been so fractured by the repetitive cycles of forgetfulness that you are unaware that you are even imprisoned, let alone that there is a key! But the keys are returning with the keepers. For there are seekers and there are keepers. The seekers are unaware; blindly seeking something that they feel deep inside is missing. They seek desperately to find themselves, find information and knowledge to give themselves some kind of clue, some kind of direction, some kind of purpose. Then there are the keepers. The keepers KNOW something is missing, they know that there has been enslavement; they know that this world isn't quite what it seems. They know that what they are meant to be finding is not anywhere outside of them.

They appear to be seeking, but they are the ones who hold keys of knowledge within them. The more they try to seek it outside of themselves, the more they falter. Their souls are screaming to rise up, *to wake up, to unleash the knowledge they contain within. The key to finding their own keys within them is **remembering**. And these very words are designed to assist them. For the keepers are the souls who have not been ensnared in the karmic cycles. They are souls who have completed their personal ascensions during their earthly incarnations and who have returned to assist the planetary ascension wave.*

They have the knowledge within them of worlds within worlds, and deep within them they understand the illusion of death. They understand that they are not here to consume as much as they can without passion and purpose. The mediocre life that they see in others around them almost infuriates them. They are programmed with meaning and purpose and they feel that they are to bring something to this world. They have a notion that they are destined for big things, what your mental health field describes as grandiosity. For those of you recognising what we speak of, hear this and hear it clearly. You ARE here for big things. The flames that fan your grand ideas of change must be kept alight. Not only for your own survival, but for those around you who are your brothers and sisters. You understand this in the core of your being. The laws of the cosmos reside within you.

The law of three, the trinity, states that for anything to migrate from spirit to matter, i.e. to come into form, must be stated three times. The law of divine free will states that all beings residing in the third dimensional plane have free choice and power to choose their own direction. Anyone or anything that comes to present itself to you, physical or non-physical, must be challenged three times to reveal its truth.

The real protection you will ever need is to understand this in its entirety. If truth is what you are seeking and you want to know if what you are receiving is of unconditional light and unconditional love, then challenge it on the level of the trinity by asking three times if the entity or information is in your highest and best interest. This, dear ones, is the real meaning of you saying, 'Everything happens in threes'.

And for those seekers looking for something more tangible, here's something we prepared a little earlier ...

Protection Affirmation

I am of unconditional light and unconditional love. Across all dimensions, time and space and all directions, I am protected. I stand in my truth without fear. I stand in my being without interference, for when I stand in truth, light and love, fear cannot be. I trust completely that I am looked after, provided for and always in the right place at the right time for my highest being.

Notice that we don't say highest 'good'. Nothing is good or bad; drop the judgement, for when you judge you are limiting the experience you need for your development. Develop-meant ... you are meant to develop yourself through experience. Think of adversity as your university of learning. True learning will not come from some academy or institution. Let life be your teacher and your higher self be your guide.

Armed with the Key of Awareness, it's time to obtain the Key of Awakening.

The Key of Awakening

**The real question is not whether life exists after death.
The real question is if you are alive before death.**

Osho

I'm 33 and I'm having a vision. It's not my first and won't be my last. I'm feeling distressed about the direction of my life as I sit on my somewhat comforting purple suede lounge. The vision appears as if I'm watching a movie in front of me in a holographic image. I see myself as a soul before I was born. It looks like I am in some kind of mid-heaven space and I am walking down a corridor, except I'm not walking because I don't have a body yet.

It appears that I am pure consciousness. I am floating, moving through a hallway and I'm on a mission. I'm on my way to choose my parents! As I float down the hallway, I come to a section where there are doorways on each side, left and right. I travel through the left doorway and find seven women standing in a line. They look like they are in the army, completely silent and staring blankly straight ahead. Above each woman there is a holographic screen with a movie playing of her life. I can see their whole lives playing out with prominent scenes in quick succession. I stand in front of each woman, briefly looking at their lives. I am aware that I know

31

exactly what I am looking for. When I find the woman who appears to have more painful and traumatic scenes compared to the others, I stand in front of her and mentally make my selection by saying 'this one' in my mind.

Then I float across the corridor to the other side to enter the other doorway in search of my father. There are seven men standing there; blank stares on their faces like robots, just like the women. I watch the holographic screens playing of their lives. I'm aware that I need to find the corresponding man that would match my mother's lifespan and ultimately marry her. When I believe I have found him I pull the holographic video images together with my fingers, as you would see in a sci-fi movie.

As the two screens merge, they appear to jump time, providing a new scene as I see their lives play out together. I feel pleased with myself, as if I have just won a game of bingo. I watch as they marry and their children are born, four sons and then me. In a series of flashes I see myself being born and all the experiences that I would have. I see the difficulty, I see the pain. Not only of myself but of my family. I see fighting, violence, poverty and despair. I see my loneliness, my confusion. I see my mother's trauma and her going in and out of psychiatric hospitals and I see my family falling apart with my parents splitting up. I see myself grow older with deep psychic pain, turning to alcohol and drugs to ease the insurmountable pain that I do not understand. I see myself getting off drugs, finding a new way of life and working in the drug and alcohol field to help others do the same. The scenes bring me up to my current age at the time, 33. I try and see forward but the scenes start becoming cloudy, and I somehow know I am not meant to see any more than this.

I notice that I am full of excitement and quite proud of myself, almost like a kid who has baked their first cake. I watch as I clap my hands together, excited about the new journey I am about to embark on. I feel I have chosen the perfect ingredients for my life to come. I have a wise knowing that everything I'm about to live, all those experiences I am about to have, are going to be needed because I am first going to have to walk in the shoes of those that I would be helping.

Then I'm back in this reality, on the purple suede lounge. I breathe a sigh of relief and think, "Oh, so things are going exactly according to plan, then!"

When we come through the birth canal we forget where we came from and everything before we got here. I believe it is our destiny to make a return journey in our consciousness, to remember fully where we came from, why we're here and what we're doing. Yet, we live in a world that seems to be designed to eradicate any memory, suppress any information or education around the true nature of the spirit and the soul. No wonder it's like a jigsaw puzzle and a maze to try to find our way back to the truth and to the light.

This particular vision for me formed part of an awakening which led me to really stand in my purpose. Awakenings form the road maps for you to do so. For you to rise above your fears and live a life of freedom, empowerment and excitement that is available to you, you must first be aware and awake. Do you think you could get even a small fraction of things done in your everyday life if you were to do it while being half-asleep? Of course not. You would be bumping into things, making mistakes, and creating chaos that would need to be cleaned up later.

It sounds absurd that we would even attempt to do things while not yet fully awake, but this is how a lot of us have been operating, on an autopilot level, unconsciously walking through life until somewhere, somehow, something comes along to jolt us awake, and depending on the type of jolt, the awakening can result in the following initial reactions:

◊ Oh wow, I'm in total awe

◊ Oh shit, what is going on?

◊ Oh my God, am I going crazy?

◊ Oh man, I can't compute this, I'm going back to sleep.

Contrary to popular belief, awakenings are not reserved for those meditating on some mountaintop or in some darkened room, swaying and making chanting noises. There might be a number of things that occur in our lives that start the process of awakening; it could be a loss, death of a loved one, traumatic event, near-death experience or any real major life change that causes us to stop, ponder and question the direction of our lives. If handled well, a lot of genius, creative moments can be the outcome of these awakenings. They can jolt us out of the experience seat and into the front row where we can take stock and become our own objective observer.

However, the awakening that seems to come out of nowhere and is not related to any figural experience can really be the thing that causes you to question your sanity. These awakenings occur in highly sensitive souls who are more sensitive to collective consciousness and wider field energies. Because they are tuned into these energies, the evolutionary and planetary awakenings that are occurring are affecting them on deep levels, often out of their awareness.

Following are some of the experiences that can be misdiagnosed or referred to as some kind of disorder. They are all similar in nature, but I have taken the time to describe each one individually so that you can see the many different ways in which awakening can occur. Rather than seeing these experiences as a disorder, when understood and integrated they can foster and catapult us into great, deep spiritual truths that empower and enlighten our path, so we are not sleepwalking and trying to fumble our way through the dark.

Disorder or awakening – same same but different!

Existential Crisis

Oh shit, what is going on? An existential crisis is a situation where you question the very foundation of your life. Your very existence. In trying to find some purpose or value to your life, you may question how you fit into the world, what you're meant to be doing and what you're really living for. It could also be referred to as a mid-life crisis, but many people of different ages will have a crisis like this at some point in their lives.

This process, although *called* a crisis, is really a rite of passage. If this experience can't be processed, however, it then becomes a crisis, resulting in feelings of depression, inability to sleep, dissatisfaction with life and acting out in strange ways that aren't typical. The reason why a middle-aged man or woman may suddenly make major life changes – for example, by getting a flash car, ending their 20-year marriage, or starting a rock band – is that they have suddenly woken up to the harsh truth that they've been living a life that someone else has carved out for them; that they haven't really been consciously doing what they really wanted. All of a sudden they might look mad and selfish to those around them, but all their out-of-character behaviours are really an attempt to restore order in their life (albeit in a desperate, OMG-is-it-too-late manner).

If you could rewind time, and stopped to really think about what it is you really wanted to do, what you wanted to experience and how you wanted to be, would you choose to do that? I'm guessing most of you would say yes, but chances you are you may not have been allowed to form your own opinions or decisions, and were influenced to choose what was expected of you.

It's Time to Grow Up!

**Listen to your being. It is continuously giving you hints;
it is a still, small voice. It does not shout at you, that is
true. And if you are a little silent you will start feeling
your way. Be the person you are. Never try to be another,
and you will become mature. Maturity is accepting the
responsibility of being oneself, whatsoever the cost. Risking
all to be oneself, that's what maturity is all about.**

Osho

The maturation process is something a lot of us miss and I have helped a lot of people with this in my therapy and healing practice. The real definition and process of maturity is taking all of the beliefs that you've ever been given and questioning them to see whether they are beliefs that you would like to consciously adopt.

If you think about it, a lot of people never really experience this process of going through everything that's been handed down to them to see if it's a good fit! We often try jeans on for size, but not beliefs. Let's face it – we are not really encouraged to choose what to believe. They are like those hand-me-down clothes we accept with a smile because we are expected to.

If you 'mature' responsibly, you may begin to question your faith or investigate certain traditions or beliefs to see whether they fit for you. Is marriage for you; is a Muslim god or Christian faith what you want to follow? Do you want to own a house and have a family or do you want to explore the world and live freely, experiencing as much as you can as you go along? Have you been taught to believe that you can't choose all of this? In reality, all these questions form a process of healthy self-inquiry, but it can feel like a confusing internal crisis.

When you overcome a crisis, you rise like the phoenix from the ashes, better than what you were before you entered the flames.

Transformation is about alchemy. If you want to transform your life, the questioning process is a necessary component. Ironically, when you or others around you question the *questioning* and interpret your search for meaning as a 'crisis', you may find yourself stuck. You may be prevented from completing the transformation by people around you who think you've gone crazy. They may also pressure you into conforming back to the way you were if your new beliefs conflict with theirs. Although your authentic self is attempting to emerge, you may feel crazy and frustrated. Confusion, pressure and stress take their toll and medications may become an option to deal with everything. If you decide to collude with those around you and just 'behave' in the ways you are expected to, you may initially feel happy but what you have done is DEPRESSED your own spirit, your own soul's calling, and you will become depressed once again until another *crisis* comes along to awaken you again.

Normal and healthy	Not-so-healthy but normal
Questioning what's normal	Not questioning why certain customs are there and accepting things at face value
Questioning the status quo	Accepting what is given
Investigating belief systems and models and other cultures	Not choosing what to believe in or researching own culture, customs or beliefs
Making conscious decisions on what to believe	Believing in what you're told to believe
Trying different ways of being	Not attempting to deviate from what is expected by others
Asking why	Not asking why and just following others' directions and orders for what's best

Spiritual Awakening

Spiritual awakenings are not all peace, love and sunshine. A real awakening shifts you out of your worldview seat, flips it upside down, back-to-front and suddenly makes you feel alone, knowing the truth that others can't see.

Me

Picture a champagne bottle here. I like to describe this kind of awakening as one where your head pops out of your arse! Pop! Probably not the best visual, but you get the idea. Suddenly the world doesn't revolve around you and all your needs. You may suddenly have an interest in the lives of others, an intense connection to nature and animals and an interest in what is happening in the world. The awakening of the spirit is a representation of connection to the whole. There is a connection to the flow of the universe that becomes an intuitive reaction. Awareness of synchronicity is heightened and often connection or awareness of a divine universal force can be felt.

Signs that you're experiencing a spiritual awakening can include a newfound ability to just let things go, being in the flow, feeling more frequent and higher levels of happiness, appreciation and gratitude. You may notice you're more spontaneous rather than behaving based on fears from past experiences. You find yourself being able to be more present, enjoying each moment and losing your tendency to worry. You may lose interest in conflict and interpreting the actions of others. You might stop judging yourself and gain the ability to love without expecting anything in return. Everything feels free and joyous! Who needs drugs, right? Or champagne, for that matter. I'll have what she's having!

If a spiritual awakening happens rapidly, it appears as a complete personality shift. For sensitives, the increased happiness may look like mania; the carefree attitude in someone who was once a constant worry-wart might appear as carelessness. The shift may cause others to wonder what the hell has gotten into you. Some well-meaning professionals conditioned in the art of pathologising may even think you're experiencing mania and going into some phase of an illness that must be controlled and suppressed.

When allowed to take its course, a spiritual awakening can enrich your life. It may feel as though you are reborn, with a completely new perspective and an inner shift in the core of your very being. It's not always comfortable, though. Friendships and relationships with family may feel different to you and you may want to cull the friends who you used to resonate with but now feel a disconnection. Your family may suddenly feel suffocating, especially if they're not welcoming of your sudden changes. You may try to fit back in because you feel different, and the basic human nature of your need to belong kicks in. There is then a subconscious attempt to shut down the awakening. However, once awake, it's hard to go back to sleep, and the suppression causes a cycle of anxiety and depression. Just because your spirit has awakened, doesn't mean you've made it. The journey is not yet complete and just because the universe wants to kick your butt along to really remember who you are, spiritual awakenings often lead to ...

The Dark Night of the Soul

The dark night is where the awakening process turns into a journey that awakens the soul. It's aptly called a *dark night*, because it's a journey you must finish on your own without any outside help. Think of being locked out of your house at night with no phone to call anyone or light to see with! It is a calling to integrate everything that you have discovered in your spiritual awakening and work out how to walk in this new way of life. It's a realisation that real truth and answers *must* come from within; that real guidance is between you and your maker. The deeper meaning of life and your place in it becomes your focus in this stage.

The duration of the dark night of the soul will depend on how long you take to integrate and accept your spiritual awakening. Dark nights of the soul can be difficult because you may suddenly feel like you're the only one who is awake to others around you. It might even feel like you're on the set of the TV series *The Walking Dead*! As you shift in vibration and perception, a deeper awakening experience continues. Everyone experiences this in different ways, but you might experience an increase in arguments, feelings of dissatisfaction, irritability and discomfort for no particular reason, or a significant change in beliefs where, for example, some of the ideas you viewed as crazy conspiracy theories suddenly appear to have some truth in them.

A lot of courage is needed to walk through this process and come out the other side. It requires you to lose the fear of what other people think, to become your own leader; to not be afraid to be different, even if it costs you the respect of friends and family who do not understand your sudden change. The dark night of the soul can be a painful process, because the pain of remaining the same often outweighs the pain of change. You find that you must choose the lesser of two evils, both of which appear to bring discomfort and pain.

The dark night of the soul often challenges you to become aware of your ego. Often, those who go through an awakening become judgemental of others and sometimes the entire human race. The frustration causes a lot of anger to rise within as you think, "What the fuck is really going on with this world?" It is at this time that your perception may become skewed as you look outwards at all the ways in which the world is fucked up. How people are ignorant, how people hurt each other. The way out of the woods with this one is to search inside yourself to find out how you are operating in the world. If you're honest with yourself, you will often find that the very things you are judging, are operating in you. You might be selfish and self-centred, or you may be hurting others but are blind to it because of your own egotistic righteousness.

There is no light at the end of the tunnel.
There is only you, YOU ARE THE LIGHT.

Unknown

If this resonates with you, it is important to focus on the end result. Once through the process and the fears are overcome, the very liberation of your soul makes up for what you may think you have lost. The opposite can actually occur. Instead of experiencing rejection, you may be admired by others for your audacity and your courage (a.k.a. wings) in your new way of being! This is, after all, how all great leaders are born. Great leaders are not followers; they pave a new way forward which is always rejected by others at first! Remember, you've got this. There's a great leader within you attempting to emerge; let go of fear and embrace the change with both hands.

Ego Loss

A common component of the dark night is ego loss. Ego is a widely misunderstood concept and loving yourself really does get a bad rap! Ego, though, is really about deep-seated fear. Your soul knows that fear is an illusion, and as the planet is raised to new levels of truth, more and more people are experiencing ego death.

An ego death is a complete loss of subjective self-identity. Your ego is shaped by your experiences, your likes, dislikes, your insecurities, fears, wounding – it's all part of the ego. You might find your identity through your status in life, whether it's being a husband, a wife, mother, brother, etc. Or it might be the status of a career, whether you're a lawyer, an accountant or a teacher, for example. Ego death can be seen as the loss of attachment to these titles. It has been said amongst many ancient cultures and spiritual texts that the ego must die for enlightenment to occur. Carl Jung viewed psychic death as "a fundamental transformation of the human psyche".

Losing your ego, or ego death, is not really about your ego dying but a falling away of the shadow self and emerging into a new way of being with the lens of distortion off. It's a melding into the truth that you are not 'you' in your ego, but that your ego is a part of you. Transcending duality and your ego's grip on you is the pathway to develop unconditional love and acceptance for all things. This transcendence helps you see the way in which the universe is mirrored back to you through your own perceptions.

Ego loss is a process, not an event. It often consists of what is referred to as 'Satori', which is a Zen Buddhist word that means 'momentary enlightenment'. Satori is a small glimpse, a window experience of seeing your true nature, the divine consciousness within you when your ego is completely shed. It acts like a doorway, giving you the choice of whether you want to take the blue or red pill. It can be an enlightening or an earth-shattering experience. Many people feel great depths of depression and darkness through this process as though they want to give up, and they lose the will to continue being as they are. They are not sure why these feelings have arisen but their soul is calling for them to rise and awaken. It's not an easy process.

We have two alternatives: either we question our beliefs – or we don't. Either we accept our fixed versions of reality – or we begin to challenge them. In Buddha's opinion, to train in staying open and curious – to train in dissolving our assumptions and beliefs – is the best use of our human lives.

Pema Chödrön

It can be scary as your point of view about yourself changes. For example, you may find that you knew yourself well, but realise you have been selfish when you thought you were being kind. You may start to see the ways you operate within interpersonal relationships and have a complete shift in self-perception. The illusion of fear and separation starts to become apparent as you see the multitude of ways that you are connected to yourself, with others and the world at large. You may question the fabric of reality itself. It can feel like that comfortable rug you've been standing on has suddenly been pulled out from under your feet.

Lots of people experiment with psychedelic drugs to experience an ego death. They are searching to transcend into a hyper-aware connectivity to all things to have an awakening experience. But there are those of you out there who have had abilities to go into altered consciousness at will and haven't known this about yourself. When an ego death happens in this situation, it's hard to understand what you are experiencing. You may now see the reality of a crazy world and wonder what is behind it all, with a myriad of questions beginning with 'why'. As Morpheus said to Neo in *The Matrix*:

> *You're here because you know something. What you know you can't explain, but you feel it. You've felt it your entire life, that there's something wrong with the world. You don't know what it is, but it's there, like a splinter in your mind, driving you mad. It is this feeling that has brought you to me.*

Starseeds (a subject I will discuss later on in this book) often have this experience built-in like a claircognizance from an early age. As a teenager, I would often retreat into my inner world, writing poetry to help myself. It was though I was expressing the undeniable truth that I held resonating in my very cells that I could not form into words or dare tell anyone. I wrote this when I was just 17; seven years before the *Matrix* films came out. Some of you might relate.

What is Real?

What is real in this hyped-up world?
Why do I feel the inclination to shut my eyes
And imagine something distant and different
A world that does not distort the truth with lies.
What is real if it's all make believe?
Why so much existence of fantasy?
Maybe to cover reality of a cold world
A selfish world. Me for I and I for me.
What is real in a mixed-up mind?
Influence and experience block the passage
Shades of emotion different to the program
Are we individual or part of the crowd so massive?
What is real, is reality fixed
Manufactured by power and control?
If so, what is real will be answered
For me, only from within my soul.

Spiritual Emergency

Another term for the *crisis* part of a spiritual awakening is 'spiritual emergency'. This term was first used by Stanislav Grof and his wife Christina in the early 1970s to describe a stage in life where individuals become aware of their specific spiritual nature. They were aware that a spiritual awakening can lead to a temporary stage of crisis. Spiritual emergencies can last minutes, days or weeks, but always end with a positive outcome if they are not interrupted. Like the other awakening processes, not interrupted may mean not being shut down by chemical medications, or judged by yourself or people around you as nonsense.

If you experience an emergency, you may go through streams of consciousness and non-stop synchronicities that lead you down a rabbit-hole of spiritual exploration and soul-searching. Psychic phenomena may begin to happen, which can make you feel crazy or a bit like the world and all your experiences are a giant jigsaw puzzle where the pieces don't seem to fit.

You may go into an altered state of consciousness during an emergency. The 'emergency' part often refers to the somewhat compulsive and compelling urges to explore experiences and information and act on internal guidance. Often this guidance is not in any reference to this life, or it can be confusing or out of character. Hearing guidance and having visions can be part of it, which feels crazy if you haven't experienced anything like this before, but the tipping over into other worlds is simply your soul searching for answers. A spiritual emergency can often look like a psychosis, where deeply buried ideas and processes are coming up from the unconscious into the conscious with no explainable reference point in the here and now.

Kundalini Awakening

Kundalini is a Sanskrit word meaning serpent power, which stands for higher self or the power of consciousness. It is regarded as a feminine, divine force within that is very powerful. It's not something that can be measured by medical science, because it is an energy that lives in the subtle bodies. The seven subtle bodies are layers which exist around the physical body. They create your aura and can be seen as the vehicle of consciousness with which one passes from life to life. They can be regarded as the bodies of the soul. Medical science only looks at the physical which, on a soul level, isn't really realistic. Forgetting the rest of these bodies is like having a Snow White with no dwarves! We can't have a Snow White with no dwarves! However, they are called subtle for a reason, because they can't be seen with the naked eye.

It is said in many eastern traditions that enlightenment is when the kundalini is fully awakened in the body. Kundalini is usually asleep and said to be coiled on herself three-and-a-half times in the base of our bodies. At some stages and in some individuals, this kundalini energy awakens and aligns all of our chakra points. In many eastern traditions, people meditate for years and years in an attempt to awaken it. But what most people don't understand is that kundalini can often awaken spontaneously during a healing or as a result of a profound emotional shock; a personal crisis, separation, serious accident, life-threatening illness or death of a loved one.

The subject of kundalini awakening has been kept hidden for a long time. This is because it was usually reserved for esoteric teachings between spiritual masters and their students, because an inappropriate awakening of the kundalini energy can be problematic. It is usually advisable that a spiritual teacher who understands this energy is there to assist the person. It has been said that most kundalini awakenings do not happen in full. Physical symptoms of kundalini rising affect the central nervous system, with each person experiencing different things. Kundalini rising may feel like back pain or cramps, shaking or quivering in different parts of the body, sudden rushes of energy, explosions of light in the brain and tingling or numbness in various body parts, increased sexual energy, spontaneous orgasms, sudden new insights, or frequent changes in sensory perception.

You may also hear tones, have changes in sleep and eating patterns, hyperactivity, pressure in your skull, visions and other mystical experiences, and you may also find yourself spontaneously crying or laughing. Sounds like madness, doesn't it!

Everyone is different. The point is that when you are experiencing things like this, you may feel crazy unless you know what is happening. I didn't know what kundalini was until I was guided to research it after I had a spontaneous orgasm while doing a chakra meditation. Lucky me! Soon after I had incredible bursts of energy that made my head rattle from side to side, almost rotating like chopper blades, and vibrations through my whole body. I seriously felt like I was going to fly off!

Kundalini awakenings that are completed in full are referred to as achieving self-actualisation, Christ consciousness, Buddha nature or the gift of the Holy Spirit.

It's easy to see that the pathway to enlightenment, which can connect you to beautiful ways of unconditional love and connection back to source, can be regarded as a disorder; something to be drugged and dumbed down. This is where chaos ensues and your integration of spiritual evolution could be halted. Spiritual evolution is a beautiful journey to be embraced and understood and integrated.

Remember to shift your perception when you're feeling mad, crazy or unwell. Do your research, get support if you realise that you are experiencing a spiritual process. It's your choice about how you interpret your own experience, disorder or awakening. Same same but different.

The Pleiadians on Awakening

Your awakening is in fact your growing up. It's your maturation process in action. Some of you think, "oh look, I've awakened", but you're still in your ego; awakening is but the first step in a process. You don't wake up in the morning and think, "oh I'm done now, I've arrived" – no!

First step is the awakening of the spirit, that you are not singular; you are a part of the whole. You see and feel the spirit within yourself and the connection to other living consciousness that is alive. This is why you feel all-live. When you connect to all living things, you see that you matter and all things matter. You begin to care for yourself and the reflection that is you through all that you connect with. You connect with nature, animals and people in a way you haven't ever before, feeling joy like never before and you feel fresh, and so you should as this is a new part of you that has emerged. This stage is not an event, it's a process, and just like a lotus flower opening to the sun, it does so slowly. Your spirit takes its time to awaken and comes in many forms as you navigate your way through life.

WHAT DO I DO IF I DON'T FEEL LIKE I'M SPIRITUALLY AWAKE?

Look to where you are dependent on others for your survival and happiness. If you are looking for others to take care of you in some way – not as in caring or providing, but where in your relationship you are 'dependent' on them or on that particular thing for you to feel free. You see, your freedom must come from you; you cannot form a relationship with you and the world around you unless you disconnect and be your own human. The spirit within you is what truly sustains you; the spirit that is connected to the one spirit of all is what awakens you. What blocks you from connecting to that is your connection to the other. We mentioned that this is a maturation process, yes? Well, consider it as though you have to let go of your mother's apron strings. This is where girls become women and boys become men.

The next step is the awakening of the soul, and my, oh my, this is an interesting ride. This is where you realise that your eyes are for looking in, not just out. This is where your awareness expands out beyond all living things and you experience a shift of perception. You begin to see that not only are you connected to creation but that you can create for yourself. The religious would call this blasphemous – after all, there is only one creator, God. The concept of one creator is hilarious to us, and anyone who has had their soul awakened knows we are all creator gods. The reason for the hilarity – and we are not mocking you – is the plain and simple fact that you decided to come here through the birth canal. There's your first myth busted there! The typical human mindset is that you were created by your mother and father. Nope. They were vessels and channels for you to come through on. They provided you the passage to enter this place and you consciously chose them. We demonstrate this point to show you the fact that you are a powerful creator who has influence over your surroundings and your reality. What is real for you is what you choose it to be. When your soul awakens, you become very aware of how you are interacting with yourself and the world around you, and you are care-full, because you know you're the one actually creating the circumstances that you are experiencing.

DOES THAT MEAN I'M IN CONTROL OF EVERYTHING?

There is a difference between creation and control. Con-troll is manipulating things and people to get what you want; you are conning another and reducing them to a 'troll' status. This is in fact breaking one of the greatest universal laws of free will, where all beings have free choice, and brings great negative karma. Karma is not punishment; it is merely cause and effect. This control happens a lot in human interaction and is the source of great distress for many. We could speak on this topic alone at great length. However, in general, creating is about asking and receiving and trusting and allowing. Controlling is about forcing and comes from fear. Creation comes from faith. You have been raised in the belief that without control there is chaos. The opposite is true – where there is control, there is chaos.

Armed with the Key of Awakening, it's time to obtain the Key of Vibration.

The Key of Vibration

Everything in life is vibration.

Albert Einstein

A young guy came to see me after hearing of my work and my views regarding entities and mental health. He had been hearing voices for a few years and had been hospitalised several times and told he had a psychotic disorder. I spoke to him briefly before he came to see me and intuitively knew he was using drugs. When he came in, he appeared to be calm and receptive. As he began speaking to me about his problems and the voices that were haunting him, I noticed that he appeared to be quite coherent, clear in his speech and with no apparent disorganised thoughts. I scanned his energy and could not see or feel any entities around him.

I asked him to check in with himself and to tell me if he could hear any voices speaking to him presently. He paused for a moment, scratched his head and said, "No, there's nothing there now". He looked very confused and he wasn't the only one! I double-checked with him again. "So, for the last five years you've been hearing voices continually and now they've stopped?" He said yes. I asked him when they stopped. He paused to think, and still looking baffled, said, "As soon as I walked in your front gate".

51

Like a flash in my mind's eye, I saw earthbound entities flying off him, unable to stay attached to him as he walked through my gate and onto my property. "Of course," I thought. "They've been locked out." When he came to see me I made sure, as I always do, to put an energetic cleansing and protection extending to the fence line perimeter, which allows only the vibrational energies of unconditional love and light to be present. It is something I do regularly, especially when seeing clients in my own home. That day I had spent extra time doing specific sacred geometry protections because I knew that if he had a drug problem, there would most likely be trickster earthbounds around him. It was clear to me that the laws of vibration were at play here. Because these entities were a lower vibration and did not match the frequency protection I had set, they had no choice but to leave him be! Who needs ghostbusters when you have a high vibe protection! I then explained to him why exactly it was that his voices had gone. I did some healing work with him and taught him some personal protection work. But I had to warn him and explain that in order for the voices to remain stopped, he needed to stop his ice use. Once he gained support to cease his ice use, only then could we begin addressing the other underlying emotional causes of his imbalance.

The Real Dangers

All thoughts are vibrations that create a resonance, a frequency in which we operate. This resonance operates in your emotional body and creates a sonar signal that draws the same vibration to you. Your vibration affects your perception and vice versa. In order to raise their vibration, many people who experience mental health symptoms attempt to self-medicate through the use of illicit drugs and alcohol, seeking relief. There are also those seeking awakenings through the use of plant medicine via sacred ceremonies. There is mass communication about the dangers of drugs, while a shroud of mystery often remains around the dangers that operate in the non-physical realms.

Drugs put holes in your auric field and open up your crown chakra to all the non-physical realms, both higher and lower. It's not picky! This is because the addiction process itself brings in things from the spirit world that will destabilise you. If you form a dependency on a substance, you are actually inviting in entities that are also addicted. It really is like chucking a psychic party where you're inviting non-bodied beings in to join you.

Frequencies are actually matched at the level they commenced within your intention. For example, out of your need and desperation to feel better, the frequency you invite in is of need and desperation. Both are very low vibrations. Your seeking to feel better can also carry low-vibe frequencies such as shame, guilt and remorse. There are many spirits and lost souls who walk among you, who live in the astral worlds and match this frequency. Those who do not understand that the world they live in is an illusion gravitate like magnets to this energy and can become attached to you. Although they are not in the living, they are still stuck in their own cycle of addiction and seeking a fix. They can merge with the person's energy field temporarily to feel the effects of being drunk or stoned. I have seen this dynamic when helping to clear clients, and also had to clear some of my own who were hanging around.

In working with teens with drug and alcohol addictions, I often saw that their vicious and violent crimes did not match their gentle natures. In some cases, their acts of violence were not remembered and happened during blackouts. These blackouts of lost time could be attributed to being possessed by these lost spirits. I highly recommend an entity-clearing for anyone who is addicted and seeking to address their addictions to ensure that these entities are not hanging around and waiting for them to get high again. I can't stress enough, though, that these entities are not workings of some dark forces or the devil, but are just lost spirits who haven't found their way home, seeking resolution in the best way they know how. I have great compassion for them, as I have helped many to cross over. They are obviously eternally grateful to at last find peace in their rightful place to continue their soul's journey.

The difference between whether drugs give you an enlightening experience into higher realms or scary realms is the intention with which you use the drug. This is the point of difference as to why some people spin out or can't 'handle' their drugs! If you are respectful and not abusing them, your frequency at point of use will be to the higher realms, and this can often lead to profound spiritual experiences which lead to awakenings. All plants on our planet have been provided to us for healing. Synthetic versions of these plants, though, change their molecular structure and lower their vibration.

Psychic Centres

I don't use all three of my eyes and open up my psychic vision unless I am working with someone who has given me permission. To take someone's choice away is a serious breach of one of the highest spiritual laws; the law of free will (or the Law of Choice). This karmic law should not be broken, but it often is. If you're naturally intuitive, or have dabbled in drug taking, you may have your psychic centre open all the time. This is another cause of lethargy, and unless you know how to be open only to higher vibrational fields, you can be a magnet to a whole array of psychic debris.

I was often confused and ungrounded at times in my own awakenings until I learnt to switch my abilities on and off. Think of it like a light switch. If you keep the light on, eventually you're going to run out of electricity or get a whopping bill! The deficit you are creating in your own energy field is what is draining you.

I have often had to create a vibrational switch or door within a client's energy field and teach them how to use it to help them find peace and clarity. I have also energetically closed the crown chakra slightly in some clients who are suddenly flooded with a rush of consciousness of awareness that is too much for them to handle and they are experiencing distress from feeling crazy.

Pharmaceuticals also close down the crown chakra energy, which helps people get to equilibrium and back into this world. It may be necessary for some as a temporary measure, but dependence is often formed and the root cause and spiritual knowledge of what they have tapped into is lost in the unknown. Those drugs, unfortunately, also put holes in the auric field for lower vibrational entities to enter. The pharmaceutical medications also cause a disconnection in *all* emotions, not just the low ones. People living on medications often report feeling better, but also feel flat and disconnected, almost as if they were watching their own life though a sheet of glass. They also shut down the senses, blocking intuition and psychic ability. Medications can of course save lives until the person can build on and develop other coping methods, and in some cases these side effects may need to be lived with as a temporary measure.

Other Extra-curricular Activities

It's important to note that entities also attach themselves in other lower vibrational activities such as pornography and sadistic violence. Again, these entities cause confusion, scattered thinking, irritability and displaced anger. A person with a really dark attachment will often behave in an aggressive manner, almost as if they are not themselves. It can also appear as a marked rise in libido, with uncontrollable and obsessive urges for sexual encounters. This is because the entity has merged energetic fields with the person.

Remember the saying, "You are who you hang around with?" Through energetic osmosis, you can be influenced to become way out of character. Imagine if your parents were psychic mediums? "Hey, who have you brought home now? How many times have I told you not to hang around with that riff-raff!" Sounds like a scene out of Harry Potter!

Earthbounds can also follow you home after a sexual interaction with someone who has attachments! I once found an earthbound entity in my bedroom after they had hitched a ride home with me. I found him just standing at the foot of my bed. When I asked who he was and where he had come from, he referred to himself as a *friend* of my then partner. He was looking me up and down, checking me out, nodding his head as a sign of approval. He then tilted his head, signalling towards the bed! Smiling, he said, "How about it?"

I know, right! Can't blame the guy for trying! He went on to say that my boyfriend wouldn't mind sharing me! Oh, the nerve! While holding back my laughter – not successfully, I might add – I told him that although I was flattered, there would be no fun and games in the bedroom because he was in fact dead. He appeared amused, laughing away, and said, "Listen, love, in all the years I've been knocked back, that has to be the most original knock-back line I've *ever* heard". I asked him what year it was, and he said 2006. I had to explain to him that it was 2014 but he didn't believe me, so I called for spiritual back-up and helped him find his way.

Co-morbidity

Because addiction is categorised as a mental illness in the DSM, co-morbidity is a term that refers to people who have been diagnosed with a mental illness and an addiction. There is great debate about whether mental illness causes addiction or vice versa. I see them as one and the same, just running parallel to one another. Same same but different.

There are currently many people sitting in psychiatric institutions who have been misdiagnosed with psychiatric disorders after experiencing drug-induced psychosis. What puzzles me is that people who present to mental health institutions are not asked about any drug use whatsoever, and seem to be more focused on what drugs they will be dispensing. The assessment process does not factor in drug-induced psychosis because it's a one-way street of treatment, rather than a consideration of the cause. Ironically, the drugs given to patients foster dependence in the physical body also, inviting more visitors from the astral planes and so the merry-go-round continues. When medications don't work, the doctor may say, "Hmm, let's up your dose", or put you on a different medication.

Let's take a step back and think about this. It's a drug; the body develops a tolerance, and so it needs more. It's a natural part of the drug-taking process, but what you may get told is that you must be sicker than they thought, or your brain chemistry is out of whack and you must need more help. The drug *treatment* itself is often not seen as the problem.

For every drug that is made synthetically in a lab by the pharmaceutical industry, there is a natural alternative that a plant has already derived from nature. I discovered through speaking with plant spirits that they have a consciousness of their own and can advise the correct dosage and the various ways in which they can be used. Sounds magical, right? That plants can speak. But don't go telling that to a psychiatrist; "So I was talking to this plant and it said I should take it twice a day ..." Not a good look!

Sickness, especially of the mental health kind, is not often seen in indigenous communities. Ancient knowledge held in indigenous communities includes understanding of the wisdom of plants. They treat them with reverence and hold them as sacred. Mother Nature has provided us with everything we need to allow us to heal. All indigenous communities know that if you pillage the land and its resources, there are certain dangers and nature turns against you. They respect the consciousness, the natural laws of cycles and the balance of nature. I believe we have a lot to learn from them in healing not only the planet, but its people.

Unfortunately, ancient knowledge and healing customs have largely been lost over time due to the trauma inflicted on these communities. Government officials have often consulted with elders about their plant use, allegedly operating in goodwill, but have come back later only to make their use illegal. It's become part of my work to assist the reconnection to all of this knowledge. The natural alternatives, used wisely, can be incredibly healing and return a person to a greater, if not better state of functioning than they were in prior to falling into some category of mental illness.

Grounding

We are living in a time in which most of us are experiencing a mass awakening. Grounding is just as important as clearing your energy fields and raising your vibration. The rush of seeing synchronicity signs everywhere and the sudden streams of consciousness that come with awakenings can make you feel manic and unable to concentrate. It's an effort to slow down your thoughts! Often, your crown energies are expanded, bringing in your connection to the universal intelligence which is operating at a speed that your brain can't keep up with. Feelings of great importance are common and in some ways they hold truth on a soul level, and you may be accessing important and ancient truths that make you feel special, but it is important to remember that you are you here in the now, in this reality. Discernment is needed, especially if an inner voice tells you to drop everything now and go preach to the masses, for instance.

Always remember that any guidance that may cause you to be unstable is either coming from an earthbound spirit or from your ego! Walking barefoot, swimming in the ocean, eating grounding foods such as root vegetables, bushwalking, and vigorous exercise are all important to return to the body so your head is not stuck up in the clouds. Mindfulness techniques are also helpful, as long as they are connecting you to your body. Being in your body connects you to the present moment.

The Pleiadians wanted to focus on addiction for this chapter. They let me know that this was an important message when it comes to vibrational energy.

The Pleiadians on Addiction

Addiction is a disease that has been created by man. It is not a defect of the human race, but rather something inflicted upon them. Humanity has had tools for healing since its inception, and all 'drugs' derive from the plant kingdom. Plants have properties that heal in multiple ways, from working in the physical sense to providing relief of ailments and curing ailments through the realm of experience.

The plant kingdom holds great keys, doorways and portals into other worlds because awareness of such realms is indeed the medicine that is needed in order to heal. Feelings of euphoria and an undeniable sense of unconditional love for self and others are elements of experiential healing that are sometimes needed, just as feelings of almost dying are needed for those who need a bit of gratitude in their life. Everything is polarity in this duality consciousness.

How do people become addicted?

People become addicted because of the lack of knowledge and the deliberate misuse of knowledge. The ancients knew full well what could heal and what could kill you, and each precipitation point of each plant by communicating with the plants. The plant would give instruction on how much to use for each person, and usually, no two people were the same. There was no need for experiments and accidents didn't happen. These methods have been eroded over time by greedy individuals who developed a bad name for such practices by creating and selling concoctions that didn't work.

Through the eradication over time of the wisdom of ancient practices and their communities, there were other – let's call them 'greeds' – who were now in a place of power to have influence over whole communities. They played into the human nature of wanting to feel good and feel better, and created chemical versions of the plants so that they could control their distribution and use. These greeds, as their name suggests, were not interested in healing, but power and control. The true nature of natural plant-derived medicine has slowly eroded way, with only one message left in humanity's consciousness – that drugs are bad and dangerous.

An illusion was created whereby the masses believed that they could only trust professionals who had trained in the art of medicine, and the medicine men and women of ancient times became a distant memory in western civilisation. There is an interesting part here we wish to bring to your attention; 'civilisation' was formed to create civil servants, and your sovereign rights to be, live, and farm and use the natural resources this planet had to offer were taken from you. Your indigenous races and elders know this truth and the cruelty has reigned through the generations forward. But know this: the cruelty has been inflicted on all of you, the entire human race, and it is not limited to culture, race or religion. This is the great irony that we watch unfold. There is such a divide between western and eastern civilisations, between ancient and modern cultures, between blacks and whites and whilst you fall prey to these illusions, you fail to see that the same thing has happened to all of you but just in a different way – same same but different.

Addiction on a personal level is the reaching out to obtain something that can only come from within. It is a desperate attempt to find oneself. On a deeper level, it is the wise part of you seeking to find truth through the plants that are the keepers of ancient wisdom. The youth are trying to find their way through these, because deep down in the recesses of their cells and in their DNA, they know that these plants can activate knowledge of who they are, but they get trapped into using synthetic and polluted versions of what nature intended. For every plant out there on the earth is a receptor in the brain. The plants offer a chance for those receptors to open. Some of those who incarnate here have receptors open that others do not. This is what is seen as the gifted. The ones who can merge in and out of altered states at will, who from a young age can already see through the veil. They have chosen pre-birth to allow these receptors to be open so that they can anchor themselves into the place they have just come from, to ensure they are not completely lost and to remember they have chosen to come and live and this world, but remember they are not of it. This is a great spiritual saying of the eastern world. Your energetic bodies hold the truth of this.

I hope that the information above helps you to have compassion for yourself if you are someone who has an addictive nature. It may help you see that you are actually addicted to the need to seek and obtain pleasure. Once this is understood, you can be retrained in finding other ways to bring pleasure while learning the wisdom of balance.

The Ashtar Command interrupted my writing process on this chapter, informing me that they also wanted to speak about this key. The Ashtar Command are known as the airborne division of the Great Brother/Sisterhood of Light, under the administrative direction of Commander Ashtar and the spiritual guidance of Lord Sananda, known to Earth as Jesus Christ.

The Ashtar Command

You are all vibrational beings who are desperately seeking the truth that resides in you. The pineal gland, which is the seat of the soul and is connected to your pituitary gland, is your connection to the truth, but it has been attacked in several ways. Some of you are aware of how this occurs, and for those in the know, it may it serve as a reminder. For those who don't, please take heed. Fluoride, which has been polluting your water supply, is the main culprit amongst other toxic pollutants that causes the shrinking of this gland. Thyroid issues are well known now to cause depression and a whole array of symptoms, because this gland is also connected and works in harmony with these centres. These centres, when balanced, form your connection to the divine intelligence. Feeling disconnected? Tired? Overwhelmed? These are low vibes which are not in alignment to your true spiritual nature and magnificence. Seeking solutions in fields that operate on the physical will only bring temporary relief, which is an illusion.

For holistic health to occur, the energy fields in the body need to also be nurtured. The human body is an advanced machine with so many connections. Everything is vibration. And these vibrations also travel across all dimensions in time and space. This is why remote viewing is possible, as you have the ability to surf these waves of vibration. This is why vibrations of energy are still held in objects and places and felt by those sensitive to these. Your bodies hold vibrations in your cellular memory also. Every memory has an energetic imprint, and these energies cannot be ignored; what is not cleared stays to affect you in one way or another. Clearing resentments, guilt, shame and anything not of unconditional love is imperative to your vibrational health. Your vibrational health is linked to your physical health and vice versa. All your evidence-based practices are respected, but the fact that there are unseen energies to the physical eyes are your missing pieces. Have a look at the word evidense. Your specialists and experts are trying to give you answers from energy which is dense!

Your brain disorders are linked to energy centres connecting you to the divine. Suppression of symptoms disconnects you from the very divine consciousness that can heal you. The healing powers of divine unconditional love cannot be surpassed by dense energies. The key to mastering your emotional wellbeing is related to all systems in the body and all systems are linked. The separation of modalities has caused great malady; like animals seeking desperately for the one solution, when whole solutions reside in including the higher vibrational energies not found in the earthly realms. Trust and faith have healed many conditions outside of the medical establishment. Miracles do occur because of these unseen energies. More miracles are occurring not from some unseen God who has rule over your wellbeing, but from the connection with your own heart's resonance. Again we say, raise your vibration, learn about your own divine connection and miracles will occur.

Armed with the Key of Vibration, it's time to obtain the Key of Consciousness.

The Key of Consciousness

If you bring forth what is within you, what you bring forth will save you. If you do not bring forth what is within you, what you do not bring forth will destroy you.

Jesus in the Gnostic Gospels

It's 2007 and I've gone to see my therapist – as you do! I'm feeling devastated over a recent break-up. She has always had a way of sensing my state by looking into my eyes. She looks into them deeply, sensing my pain and suggests I just sit, breathe and listen. She puts a meditation CD on. I sink into my chair, eyes closed, and begin to hear the most angelic music with a harmonic chant of "there is only love". Instantly, I find myself on the edge of a cliff.

It feels so real I can literally feel the wind on my face. I look over the edge into a canyon filled with hectares of the greenest trees I have ever seen. At the bottom is a clearing to a small, vibrant blue river. It is the most vibrant blue I have ever seen and I am almost breathless at the beauty of it all.

I start to notice that there are black dust-like specks floating out of my mouth with each exhaled breath. It reminds me of the movie *The Green Mile*, where Michael Clarke Duncan, who plays the big man John Coffey, extracts dark energy from people in order to heal them. Instantly I know that the black dust is all the anger I have been feeling that week. The specks appear to be symbolic of my resentment being expelled through my breath and out of my body. When the last of it escapes my lips, I look down into the canyon and have an urge to jump off the cliff.

Considering I can feel the physical experience of actually being on the cliff, I'm surprised that I don't have any fear whatsoever about jumping. I jump without a second thought and feel absolutely amazing. Rather than a falling feeling, I start to float and merge with everything, becoming one with the sky, the trees and the water. I feel as light as a feather and inexplicably connected to all there is. I experience an overwhelming feeling of complete joy and bliss. I want the whole world to feel what it's like to have this feeling, and I look back at the top of the cliff as though the rest of the world's population is there.

I feel a great pull to go back to the top of the cliff so I can tell them all about this beautiful place I've just found. Interestingly, a quote from the Bible slots into my mind – something along the lines of *the only way to heaven is through the eye of a needle.* I feel like I am being downloaded energetically with the knowledge that there is no way that I can actually bring people into this state; that they would each have to find their own way there.

I am disappointed, but that quickly fades as I am overcome again with the feelings of bliss. Then, without wanting them to, my eyes open. I see my therapist. She is leaning forward and staring intently at me wearing a big smile on her face.

"How long have I been gone?" I ask. She looks at her watch. "About 25 minutes." I am completely shocked. It felt like my eyes had been closed for only a minute!

The bliss quickly vanishes as I begin to worry that I've wasted my session time, and I ask her why she didn't wake me up. She smiles with a look of awe on her face. "Well, because you looked so happy! Wherever you went, it was absolutely beautiful." She explains that she had been watching my facial expressions change in great detail and could see how peaceful and happy I was. The rest of the session was spent with me describing my experience and realising that all my anger from that week was already gone. As I was leaving I joked with her that she probably should have paid me for that session!

At that time in my life, I had no reference point for what enlightenment was. When I described my experience to others who were more in the know, they told me that what I experienced resembled enlightenment, which is what spiritual seekers try to achieve through years of meditation and yoga practice. I was impressed, but rather than enlightened, the experience left me feeling baffled and weirded out. Regardless, in times of stress I would remember that state, and return to the top of the cliff in my mind so I could jump off and feel the bliss again. It became an anchor point for me.

One day, when I was experiencing a great amount of emotional pain, I had travelled in my mind to the top of the cliff to find solace. But I found myself blocked. There was a long sheet of glass that stretched as far as my eyes could see. It continued along the cliff-front, both to the left and right, leaving me with no access point for me to jump. To say I was disappointed would be an understatement. I began panicking, trying to figure out a way to get across. I'll be honest, I had almost become addicted to the bliss feeling, like it was a drug. In my mind I began to ask why I was being blocked and then, as if by magic, holographic images that were like photographs of traumatic scenes in my life appeared as imprints in the glass.

Standing there, feeling perplexed, trapped, and somewhat traumatised by the images, I was wondering what to do next when suddenly a beautiful lady appeared. She had a distinctive air of grace and telepathically told me she was the ancient Egyptian goddess called Maat. She held her hand up and motioned for me to wait. She then used her index finger to point at the glass and make the shape of a door. She told me that if I was ever trying to find peace and I was blocked, I could just simply use the door. She showed me how it slid open. Problem solved! Extending her arm out, she welcomed me through. I thanked her excitedly and jumped into that blissful feeling I had come to know and love. This time, however, I floated down like a feather right to the bottom of the canyon beside the beautiful water where Maat appeared again, waiting for me. Sitting cross-legged, she invited me to sit with her so we could talk. She told me that I could join her in this way whenever I needed to. Considering that half my heritage is from Egypt, my conversations with her always felt like I was talking to a great wise grandmother.

This altered state of consciousness experience taught me that the superconscious mind can be accessed through consciousness, and what blocks us from experiencing the pure vibration of joy and bliss is often our fears and traumas.

The Superconscious Mind

The conscious and subconscious are aspects of your mind connected to your physical body, while the superconscious mind is connected to your soul or higher self and resides in a state of no time and space. The conscious mind consists of only five per cent of our awareness. The remaining 95 per cent is held in the subconscious. Deconditioning the subconscious from limiting beliefs helps you tap into your superconscious mind. These three minds when activated contain the trinity energy, which assists you into higher consciousness necessary for ascension. Tapping into the superconscious also gets us into the doorway of the Akashic records. The Akashic records are an inter-dimensional energetic field that acts as a library where the details of all lives are recorded.

The superconscious mind holds your divine soul blueprint. It's not called the superconscious mind for no reason. It's pretty super extraordinary to gain information on where you've been before you were born, why you chose to come here, why you have strong reactions to things that can't be explained in your current life, and finally you see what all those so-called coincidences were really about!

All dis-orders come from dis-ease within the mind. True healing comes from raising the level of our consciousness. Dr David R. Hawkins, a psychiatrist and expert on mental processes, is also a pioneer in spiritual teaching. Go David! His book, *Power vs Force*, demonstrates the art form of energy testing through kinesiology and the measurement of consciousness through our emotional state. Interesting to note is that the measurement results of joy oscillate at a higher vibration than love. I have a saying, "If you're not laughing, then something's amiss". I use joy as my measuring stick for how well I'm going spiritually.

Joy is the pathway to pure bliss found in the heavenly realms. With one of the last stops to enlightenment being joy, it's no wonder the Buddha was laughing his arse off! The merging of our superconscious and conscious minds can be seen as the merging of heaven and earth.

It's fair to say that raising your consciousness obviously then puts you in an *altered state*. What's important to understand, though, is that many of you enter this state unknowingly through the doorway of trauma, and here is where it gets interesting in regards to mental health.

Trauma

Traditionally, trauma is seen as something that happens to war veterans or people experiencing violent events, while childhood trauma is commonly overlooked. The mental health system looks to see what is wrong with you, rather than what happened to you. It often doesn't factor in that adverse childhood experiences (known as ACEs) are a major contributor to instability. Those who have experienced childhoods with addiction, domestic violence, and parents with mental illness are often unable to manage their emotions as adults. The best definition of mental illness I've ever come across is this:

Mental illness is the inability to handle one's emotions.

Unknown

Neglect is part of the abuse that contributes to trauma. Without any emotional validation or nurturing to assist them to assimilate their experience, a child is experiencing trauma. A child needs to be seen, heard and felt. Humans are mean-making machines, designed to make meaning from our experiences. Without support, it's like walking the earth alone. What children need most of the time for healthy development is not taught in education systems or learnt by parents. This is why our self-development and self-help industries are booming – repairing that disconnection and missed experience from the past.

An important question in psychiatry shouldn't be what's wrong with you, but rather what's happened to you.

Eleanor Longden

The basic dysfunctional and unspoken rule in families is to not discuss, express or feel emotions. The resulting lack of experience in how to handle personal worlds and relating to others means that issues such as addiction, relational problems and violence appear to be the outer effects playing out amongst the myriad of mental health diagnoses. Although I studied in Gestalt Therapy – a modality that focuses on holistic, relational self-awareness, rather than interpreting human behaviour from a diagnostic model – I took a keen interest in mental health based on my own life experience.

In my final year of study I wrote a paper called 'A complex PTSD approach to borderline personality disorder'. My presenting argument was based on my research, where I formed the notion that a lot of mental health diagnoses could simply be recoined as complex trauma under one banner. A complex PTSD approach offers the perspective of looking at symptoms as an *emotional injury*, or what's also known as *psychiatric injury*, rather than an illness. Trauma symptoms mimic mental illness symptoms. Hypervigilance can be seen as paranoia; depression and chronic lethargy, as well as mania, can also be seen as deeply rooted reactionary responses to not being validated or understood by others. Specialists in trauma are now fighting for a new classification to be put into the DSM, known as Developmental Trauma Disorder. Although it's a more empathetic approach when used as a therapeutic approach in counselling, I still believe *things* belong in classifieds and *labels* belong on jars.

Trauma originates from fear. Even if you don't have a mental health issue, you may be immobilised by fear. We have so many fears – fear of failure, fear of success, fear of getting hurt, fear of being vulnerable, fear of not making enough money, fear of not being happy, fear of being ridiculed or criticised if we step out of the norm. Shall I go on? I think you get the gist.

Our primitive nature in dealing with fear is the fight, flight or freeze response. When faced with fear or danger, our survival instincts kick in and we get ready to fight, get ready to run, or become completely frozen like a deer in headlights. People who have experienced a lot of trauma are stuck in an ongoing state of fear and survival. Here's where you can swap 'fear and survival' for 'anxiety and depression'! The freeze part, however, is not so well understood, and it can cause those with severe trauma to disassociate from their current reality in order to cope. Think of a bird playing dead when it's caught by a cat; it has to disassociate from life completely in order to survive!

The disassociation can be so great that the mind is tricked into believing the event didn't even happen. This explains holes in the memory from traumatic events, with people unable to remember large chunks from their childhoods. It also explains the pervasive free-floating fear and anxiety adults seem to experience without even knowing why. (It's interesting to note that these same holes in memory occur in patients who are taking anti-psychotic medications.)

Here's where things get interesting. As a result of disassociation from trauma, spiritual awakening can happen in which you enter an altered state.

It's well documented that trauma causes disassociation, where you leave your body to survive, resulting in out-of-body experiences (known as OBEs). But where does your consciousness go and why doesn't it make any sense? Think of *The Matrix* as a documentary rather than a movie and it may start becoming clearer! You have a limited set of conscious beliefs while the superconscious state is like another world altogether. It's like dreaming, but in the awake state where everything is like a puzzle. It is confusing to integrate these experiences and usually they are overlapping and make no sense, just like those dreams we have. This is because the superconscious state is not linear.

Often, accident or abuse victims report witnessing their experience as if they were watching from above or from somewhere else in the room. We're told you can't travel through time, but from a soul perspective that is exactly what happens! The light-body part of you spontaneously leaves into an altered state of consciousness, through what's called splitting or disassociation. This can happen spontaneously and cause issues. The consciousness in its wisdom leaves so that you are able to deal with what is happening to the physical body.

Here's the thing: on a soul level, when consciousness leaves the body it is free to travel to other dimensions of time and space not confined to ordinary reality. This is referred to as bi-location in quantum mechanics. Trauma essentially provides a portal into the superconscious mind, permitting you to leave the physical body and travel inter-dimensionally! The ideas of inter-dimensional travel through consciousness, although rooted in the science of quantum physics and mechanics, are ironically not something that 'experts' in the mental health system would discuss at their budget meetings!

This is what the medical field of psychiatry calls psychotic breaks or symptoms of delusion. Rather than call it psychosis, which insinuates madness, I have a term that I've used to label my own experience, which I think is much more fitting. I call it a 'multi-dimensional experience' (MDE). This leaving of the body into unknown realms looks like psychosis, but you are merely escaping your current reality and going into another one (albeit one you are taught doesn't exist as a *reality*). Complex, I know! But essentially, you're not *deluded*, you are having an MDE. Same same but different.

Accessing the superconscious mind can be likened to what happens in the movie *Lucy*. In the movie, Lucy is able to access 100 per cent of her brainpower through the drugs she ingests in her body. At one point, Lucy discusses the nature of time and life, describing how people's humanity distorts their perceptions. She tells the scientists that "time is the only true measure of human life and existence". Although it is a sci-fi film, there are parallels of truth about what happens when we access all our powers that lie dormant in our DNA; our soul's cellular memory.

Another movie from the 1990s, called *The Long Kiss Goodnight* and starring Geena Davis, shows what happens when her character has a car accident. Suffering concussion, she begins to exhibit unusual character traits and skills, which uncover the fact that she has suffered amnesia about who she really is – a highly trained assassin. She changes from being a mild and meek housewife to throwing knives and shooting guns with great precision, which bewilders her because she believes she has never had any experience doing so.

I mention these movies because dormant powers and psychic ability are not reserved for the spiritual seekers who sit for hours on end meditating; they can be obtained through experiences brought on by trauma and the use of drugs, which unwittingly catapult us into the no-time-space realms of a soul traveller. I call them the 'accidental heroes' of our time.

A Shamanic Perspective

Thinking again about some of your dreams, you may recall that in one way or another you instantly travel from one location to the next, experiencing different things very randomly. This is what psychosis or MDEs are like. Shamans know it is very possible to travel through consciousness just like you can do in a dream. *Psychosis* is therefore very similar to a shamanic journey. But with all shamanic journeys, there needs to be an anchor point to which you return with certain guidelines to ensure the soul returns safely to the body. If the consciousness does not return back to the body safely, soul parts of the consciousness can get stuck and are referred to as soul fragments or soul splintering.

Soul travel is an integral part of shamanic practice. An initiated shaman knows how to send their soul intentionally into what is called a journey. A near-death experience is yet another example of when the soul leaves the body. It's well known within the shamanic framework that the soul can travel to a spiritual aspect in another dimension, to different times and places on the earth or into other galaxies.

In my work as a crystal dream practitioner, I use the process of journeying as a tool and use a specific crystal mandala that allows the person to enter the journeying state. The journeying state can help the person get information, heal issues and work through present and past life traumas and unresolved issues. In a journey, the experiencer can see and understand that everything is consciousness. Thought forms exist in rock, plant, animal and spirit. Everything is alive.

Journeys can continue into a deeper state the more they are experienced, and often continue on from a previous journey resulting in deeper meaning and insight. Examining your own psychosis, journeys or MDEs in this way can help you see that the parts in which you may have thought you were crazy contain some deep spiritual truth.

Another common shamanic practice is to go on a vision quest, which is a rite of passage similar to an initiation process, mostly found in Native American cultures. In these indigenous tribes, young boys were sent out alone into the wilderness to connect with nature and learn from spirit. It's a boys-to-men thing, just like Jesus was reported to have done in the Christian Bible. The quest was often done alone in the wilderness, in conjunction with a period of fasting and sleep deprivation. Not eating or sleeping was seen as a natural method used to access altered states of consciousness. People around the world today are often engaging in these ancient practices. It is believed that the quest allows the soul memory to awaken.

Interestingly, a person who may be deemed to be bipolar often has a naturally reduced need for eating and sleeping where they 'tip over' into *psychosis*. From a soul perspective, what they may be experiencing is an accidental journey. Through the lens of the soul, schizophrenia can be seen as shamanic initiation or a rite of passage to enter altered states of consciousness as a calling to become a healer and retrieve information and wisdom for the collective.

Soul Fragments

The body is a temple but also a vehicle.

Me

When your soul body leaves your physical body, it can get damaged along the way. Think of your soul body as a vehicle; a spaceship, if you will, that might get knocked around during its travels. Sounds nuts, right? However, around the physical body is a *vehicle* of energy in consciousness which provides a mode of time travel! It's not crazy, it's called the mer-ka-bah; referred to as the ascension vehicle. Mer-ka-bah is three words in one deriving from Ancient Egypt:

Mer meaning 'light' which rotates within itself (a bit like a rotary engine)

Ka meaning 'spirit'

Ba meaning the 'human body'.

In Ancient Egypt, the combined meaning of this word referred to a rotating light that would take the spirit and the body from one world into another. Soul fragments can therefore be seen as damaged parts of the soul body and are often said to be left behind during a traumatic event. Remember, trauma isn't just extreme torture or violence; it is any experience of great emotional pain. Some soul parts are often left behind in old relationships that have ended due to separation or death, or are left behind at the scene of an accident. This accounts for that feeling you might get where you feel like a part of you is gone or missing. It feels as though you just can't let go of an old partner, or experience flashbacks to a traumatic scene where you might have been left in shock.

What happens if parts of your soul are missing? Symptoms of soul fragmentation include: depression; a feeling of incompleteness; an inability to move forward on an issue; lost memories; feeling like you're not in control of your life; PTSD-like symptoms; feeling like you have done everything you can but you are still stuck; memories in your past where you feel like you lost something and never got it back; and feeling like life is passing you by and you're not really a part of it. As the nature of the soul lives in the superconscious, in its attempt to seek wholeness you may experience an overwhelming compulsion to visit certain places from your past, or you may even be drawn to death through suicidal ideation because the higher aspect of you is seeking to complete itself. It is aware that parts of it are still in certain places, whether in this life or another.

Incidentally, this *compulsion* can be likened to a term that is described by one of the leaders in trauma research, Bessel van der Kolk. He coined the term *the compulsion to repeat the trauma* which describes people being drawn to experiences in which they are re-victimised.

The Soul Retrieval Process

Experiencing a soul retrieval process through an experienced healer is like bringing your rotary-powered soul ascension vehicle into the repair shop. It can help you find the missing pieces in your life and feels a bit like a coming-home party. Once the process is complete, you feel like you want to invite all your family and friends over to celebrate!

Some of the benefits experienced after a soul retrieval include: a greater ability to make decisions; a sense of being more present; an ability to move past an issue you previously couldn't; an ability to begin dealing with grief and heal the blocks that have prevented you from moving on; the beginning of a new growth or healing process; and manifesting a new relationship or job. Every person is different.

The Modern-day Experiencer

With no reference point of shamanic or ancient methods, a person who accidentally becomes the journeyer through psychosis (MDE) lives within the western medicine view that they are sick and need medication. A lot of antipsychotic medication does bring people back to this time-space reality eventually, but it leaves the journey unfinished. The dream is interrupted as if there is no conclusion and the true meaning of their experiences is subdued. They are told these experiences are not real and just the delusionary part of their illness. The recommendation is to keep taking medication in order to stop these processes from happening. (The mer-ka-bah, or soul ascension vehicle, is essentially decommissioned and put in the garage.)

Unfortunately, the shock of accidentally going into worlds you didn't even know existed, plus the experience of memory fragmentation from anti-psychotic medications, form layers of trauma which cause a further split. The judgement by friends, family and peers who avoid you because of fear and stigmatisation also contributes to a psychosis being a nightmare rather than a spiritual MDE. Medication is often a reactionary Band-Aid solution that only treats symptoms and suppresses the very nature of a soul experience that could awaken you to amazing new heights. A more precautionary treatment would be to bring back the wisdom from indigenous cultures to ensure a safe *journey* and from Ancient Egypt to teach people how to drive! That way, their experiences can be processed and their soul body ascension vehicle, their mer-ka-bah, wouldn't get damaged.

To end this epic chapter, I jumped off the cliff and asked Maat to give us her perspective on consciousness!

Maat's Perspective on Consciousness

The superconscious mind is your gateway to heaven. The bliss experienced is of the heavenly state where no pain resides; only pure love of the unconditional kind. Those who have experienced trauma in their lives have access to this gateway naturally through the healing mechanisms of the body. Wisdom has been seen by humanity as something derived from the brain, but it is indeed located more in the body. As humans, you have had the ability to leave and return into your bodies before, but this knowledge has been hidden and kept only in secret societies. It was a natural occurrence in Ancient Egypt. What was commonplace knowledge and practice for us in the human body has been lost throughout history and is now referred to as myth. When you leave your body to escape insurmountable pain, whether that is physical or emotional, the consciousness splits and becomes the observer of the experience rather than the experiencer. Think of it like watching a movie where there is violence. You are still affected by witnessing the violence, but it is greatly reduced because you are not experiencing it yourself.

*This is a natural, ancient, forgotten ability that your scientists refer to as phenomena. Your physical body is still present, and so is the conscious mind, but the emotional body has entered the superconscious realm where there are no reference points for time and space. The soul part of you can indeed travel into other realms and dimensions. 'Travel' back in our day was never limited to automobiles and planes. Because of this lost knowledge, and disbelief of these realities, your conscious mind fights to try and make sense of your experience and this is where confusion ensues. These realities **do** exist, and because the conscious mind is trying to make sense of them in the mental construct of this time-space, nothing makes sense!*

Splitting does not happen in the mind; it happens in your multiple bodies! You are in a journey between current and alternate realities, which bring in all the realms at different paces and degrees. Anyone who has experienced what your world calls psychosis or a psychedelic experience may know what I speak of. The alternate realities your higher consciousness can travel to is not limited to earth time and space. It expands into the quantum field of the soul. Suddenly you are in a reality where all your lives exist side by side and layer by layer. To use the theme of vehicles, you may view it as a multi-level car park. Each car space contains times and places and experiences that you have lived at one time or another.

Anything can happen in this world and can be a happy or terrifying ordeal according to your emotional state at the time. Your vibration will direct your experience. For example, you could be triggered into a past-life emotional experience in which you have been harmed, with no mental recall, but your fears play out in your current physical reality.

If you were persecuted in another life, the memories of this overlap into this one and the fears are projected onto the people you may know in this life. This of course makes no sense to those around you. You appear to others as being 'paranoid'. Paranoia is a fictional mental construct used to describe an emotional energetic imprint. On the opposite end of the spectrum, if you were involved in an important event in service to humanity of some sort in the soul life multi-level car park, the sense of importance overlaps into this life, resulting in the mental construct your world calls 'grandiosity'.

Perhaps you can see that without the truth of who you really are as a multi-dimensional soul, your internal worlds become full of confusion and everything becomes convoluted. Detach from this convoluted energy. It does not belong to you. You live in a convoluted universe because of myths and hidden truth. I am pleased to be given an avenue to get this information out so that ancient truth can be returned to you.

In your pursuit of truth, I will leave you with this reminder; truth is not something to be gained. Do not look for it in knowledge per se; truth is already here on your planet. It always has been. It is merely lost. And when something is lost, you only need to find it. And you will find it through the doorways of your own consciousness.

With unconditional love, Maat.

Now we have the Key of Consciousness, it's time to obtain the Key of Divinity.

The Key of Divinity

Every heart has a divine intelligence and natural guidance system. With every prayer, every meditation and every thought of love, we tune in to ours.

Marianne Williamson

Bhagavan Nityananda is an Indian guru, also known as a Hindu saint, who was referred to as having been born in an enlightened state. He was found as an abandoned infant, and even in childhood displayed an unusually advanced spiritual state. His name, Nityananda, means 'always in bliss'. I had no idea who he was until I was drawn to do a spiritual retreat in his home town in India, Ganeshpuri. This book was meant to have been finished by the time I made it there, and I was anxious about getting it finished and wondered why the hell I was trekking to India when I had an editing timeline that wasn't complete. However, the calling was so strong, I couldn't deny it.

I already know that everything happens for a reason, but I still laugh at how the universe works. I was told by the retreat leader that many people have spiritual experiences, and Bhagavan's energy was still quite palpable in the local village as he had only passed away in 1961. I first 'saw' Bhagavan on the side of the road just outside the village, standing there making a welcoming gesture as our van drove in. I had not known what he actually looked like at this stage, and I was strangely not perplexed that he appeared to just be wearing white underwear!

I later found out that he was a minimalist and non-conformist to anyone's standards, and only chose to wear this G-string cloth at the insistence of others. On the first night of my retreat there, I was visited by him in my bedroom doorway. Being 'visited' by an old Indian man in a white G-string in a non-spiritual context is weird, but being no stranger to spirit visits, I was not disturbed but fascinated. His arrival was clear from his vibration and instantly I knew I was in the presence of a wise being. I bowed my head in grace and told him that I had come to him with an open cup and asked him to teach me what he knew. He nodded and then disappeared.

I have stayed away from organised religions, like a lot of us, so my instant respect surprised me, but his air of wisdom was palpable. If I wasn't so sensitive to energy and hadn't felt his grace, I may have told him I was tired from my day of travel and to come back tomorrow when I was better rested! I'm glad I didn't, as he has become my teacher and friend. He walked alongside me in spirit, teaching me as I visited and meditated in the temples.

He appeared again on my first night back at home. He must have been on Indian time, because it was around three am and I was woken by a loud creaking door. He was standing in my lounge room and motioned for me to sit with him as he had something to teach me. This time, because we were friends, I told him telepathically that I was too tired to get out of bed, so he told me to grab my notebook from my bedside table and take notes. I was wondering why he had come. A memory then popped into my head from three months earlier, when I was told by a psychic healer that I had a new earth guide assigned to help me and that he had dark skin. Rather than tune in and speak with him myself, I assumed he was an aboriginal spirit man because of my affiliations with aboriginal culture, having been visited by aboriginal medicine men before.

He explained that *he* was the dark-skinned man and that he was the one who called me to come visit his home town. I thought, "Oh shit, of course!" Then he said, "I heard that. Don't swear; shit is a swear word". No, he didn't – just kidding. He extended his hands out and these scarab beetles appeared and he told me I was being appointed with these beetles from ancient Egypt. I sensed that they were a symbol of death and rebirth (which my research later confirmed). He told me I was being rewarded for my own personal spiritual work and that I had broken a great cycle across lifetimes of oppression and liberation. He said I was doing well in learning to trust and speak my truth.

He then confirmed for me some details of a past life of mine I had recently discovered and how this was impacting me in my life now. He told me there was some residual fear in this life still operating by way of my ongoing writing blocks. The past life he was confirming was one where I was a high priest in ancient Egypt, who was a scribe responsible for retaining and scribing ancient wisdom for generations to come. However, at the time, I was under the ruling of the great pharaoh Akhenaten. This pharaoh was responsible for bringing in a new religion where only one god was to be worshipped, rather than many, and he forbade anyone from scribing about the old religions, hoping to eradicate this history. I disagreed with him and continued to write about the many gods. To teach me a lesson and demonstrate his authority to the people of the time, the great oppressive pharaoh had me stripped and whipped in public and then locked away where I starved to death for my insolence.

I asked Bhagavan why he had come to explain ancient Egypt to me when he was from India. He explained to me that that's where he originated from as a soul, and that he was from the family of light of Christ consciousness; from a group souls whose mission was to carry on the example of enlightenment and ascension in the human body. He told me he chose to go to India as that was the only place in this modern time where he would not be shut down and locked up as insane, as the community there was open-minded and spiritual enough to know graciousness when they saw it. He also explained that his energies were then able to be anchored into the earth grid for generations forward. He then gave me some more personal advice about my current relationships and my way forward in my path and suggested that he would help me with my book. And so here he is, making an appearance!

I felt deeply grateful and as I went to thank him, he insisted that I should be thanking myself, saying, "After all, you were the one who presented yourself graciously with an open cup". I asked him if being woken up at three am was going to be a habit and he replied, "Only when it is necessary to shake you out of your own ego-driven tendencies to stay in pain, fear and grief". He was referring to the state I was in when I went to sleep. He spoke to me about my own recent experience of ego death and the emotional turmoil I had been feeling. He said that for humility to occur, we must first be humiliated. He was referring to my self-examination of my awareness of how neediness through my ego had been operating in my life. He also referred to my recent thoughts of visiting Egypt and told me it was important I go, which I later did.

I am grateful for his teachings and now, at his request, I allow myself to be a channel of his wisdom on divinity. Bhagavan, take it away ...

Divinity is in all of you, in your very nature. Divine beings are not just in the heavenly state or what is referred to as the ascended master realm. You are all on your pathway to remembering your divinity. How can you do this? Let's get practical. Look within your own ancestral lines for the karmas you are carrying forward through the generations. What has not been transmuted simply carries on. Matter does not disappear, it just moves. When someone is distressed, don't you ask, what's the matter? The matter that you cannot seem to find the cause of is often within your genes. The rest is in your DNA; your soul lives within the incarnations in which you have lived. Again, what is not transmuted in these lives carries on to the next. True healing, true soul healing, occurs on these levels, because you are not just you in this life; you have many yous in multiple lives and in many places.

Although I originated in my previous life as Bhagavan Nityananda in India, I too am from different places and carried the essence of all my collective wisdom in the one body. This is why my presence was felt by so many and respected as divine grace. You are no different to me, except your wisdom and grace lays dormant. It is in your matter within you, waiting to arise. Your malady of illness of the mind is in fact an illness of the soul. A sickness of the soul which is repressed. You are not responsible for this repression, but you are responsible for its liberation. What you have collectively repressed in the western world is merely in the reaction to the outer oppression of such subjects. But the world is far and wide. Expand your viewpoint, be open to new ideas, discover the beliefs that support others in their evolution and see if they make a good fit for you. But always know that your soul will answer you correctly every time and your body shall confirm it in signs and signals.

Those goose bumps and shivers are indicators of truth and that sick, off feeling is a feeling of deceit. Your body will show you the path to liberation and freedom to discover what really is the 'matter'. You are a divine being with your soul's wisdom held in your very cells. Namaste.

Family Constellations

When the family has been brought into its natural order, the individual can leave it behind him while still feeling the strength of his family supporting him. Only when the connection to his family is acknowledged, and the person's responsibility

seen clearly and then distributed, can the individual feel
unburdened and go about his personal affairs without anything
from the past weighing him down or holding him back.

Bert Hellinger

Along my personal therapy journey, my therapist introduced me to
a whole new level of healing called Family Constellations, created
by Bert Hellinger. She described it as healing of the soul. At the
time, I was open to anything. I loved the work and results so much
I studied it to become a facilitator. I learnt that the family and
generations before us consist of systems where there is a natural
order of love meant to flow. There are disruptions in the system
when the family members try to balance the energies present to
bring them into balance, even if that means carrying the traumas,
secrets and disowned energies in the system.

Family Constellations is a healing modality practice that reveals
the hidden and unseen dynamics at play in your family of origin.
For example, there are many cases where it has been revealed
through this work that feelings of depression and anxiety are
traced back to a child carrying the disowned heavy burden of
guilt or grief for a parent from a young age. Through a process of
facilitation, the energies can in some cases be returned to their
rightful owners in the generational line so the flow of love can be
restored.

It is deep and profound work where situations and patterns can be
transformed, where other modalities have not been able to help.
Participants in this work are selected to represent members of the
family and then placed in position (constellated) according to how
they are in relationship with one another. For example, if there are
two parents who don't speak, they might be placed facing away
from each other. The facilitator may then go and enquire with each
representative to see how they are feeling in their bodies in relation

to the other representatives in the system. The facilitator may then suggest healing statements and movements to the participants to bring back the flow of love into the system. The reactions of these representatives is uncannily accurate to real life, despite them not knowing the full story or characteristics of the person they may be representing. For example, in my first experience, the representative playing my mother said she felt totally disassociated from everything around her and was totally out of her body. She described my mother's ongoing state to a T!

What's more inspiring about this soul work is that it is often reported that the real members of the family often have reactionary shifts in nature, even though they are not present. Even mysterious physical illnesses, addiction and, of course, mental health issues can be traced to something energetic that has travelled through the family line. Deep and profound shifts are often experienced from only one session of this work. It is a great process that can only be understood when experienced for yourself.

Past Lives

Bhagavan spoke about our past lives having a great impact on us. It's hard to believe in past lives unless you have had your own personal experience. I highly suggest that you go and find out whether such things exist by seeing a past-life regressionist, crystal dreaming facilitator or hypnotherapist to see for yourself. The Quantum Healing Hypnosis Technique (QHHT), developed by Dolores Cannon, is especially helpful. A good psychic may also be able to access this information, but it's better seen for yourself so your logical mind cannot deny it.

I am more engaged in soul-healing psychic work, rather than the traditional psychotherapy I was trained in, because the healing work is just so much faster than talk therapy. I have practised and honed my skills so that I am able to complete a psychic scan in minutes and see the imbalances in all the energetic bodies of a person. This means I see the physical and mental patterns causing this, as well as the emotional ones from this life and their past. I am also able to access their Akashic records and see what contracts have been made between lives.

The number of past-life vows and oaths I have seen that are no longer serving someone in this life but have carried over is quite high. Vows such as never using psychic abilities again because of being burnt at the stake as a witch, or vows of chastity in past lives as monks or nuns. Fears and anxieties relating to large crowds, difficulties in relationships, and fears of flying and swimming that do not relate to any life experience can be traced back to past-life events. When these are seen, witnessed and transmuted with the beliefs cleared, the person can be restored to equilibrium. Likewise, past-life assets and skills can also be witnessed and called forward to be used in this life.

I'm sure you've had the experience of meeting someone for the first time and had that undeniable feeling that you know them. You know the ones, where you try to figure out where you may have met them; maybe seen them on TV, even. We old souls get it a lot. If I had a dollar for every time someone asked me if we've met before! Now I just smile and say, "Yeah – probably somewhere in a past life".

Have you noticed this is happening more often? This is because this time in history is what the ancients refer to as the meeting time, where many old souls have chosen to incarnate here to help with the evolvement of the human race, as the Pleiadians have spoken about in this book. These are examples of other non-earthly past-life histories that can affect us in the now.

For those who have made vows to never use psychic abilities again, if the vow has been made three times, then the soul who returns in the karmic wheel back into humanity will have no psychic ability at all in this life, because the rule of 'three strikes and you're out' is in effect. To assist you to have your divine right of psychic ability returned, please affirm the following:

I now, across all dimensions, time and space and in all directions, nullify and make void all vows, oaths and contracts, known and unknown, that prevent me from being in my full divine psychic power. I now claim my divine sovereign right to come back to all my senses. I call in the assistance of all energies that love me unconditionally, multiplied by nine to bring me back across time into the divine. And so it is.

Starseeds

A starseed is a type of soul who has lived many of their incarnations as a being in star systems. Starseeds have a pre-birth memory stored; they have a felt memory of what life was like before birth as a soul in their cells. They are the ones who are late, seemingly oblivious to other people's time and selfish because they are so used to being in no-time-space. They are the ones who feel the vibrations of energy but also repel, attract and transmute them on a cellular level. They make excellent healers; they are the ones who can easily leave their bodies, whether it is in meditation, or through the throes of imagination or even passion – altered states of consciousness are second nature to them. They have pre-selected a time in their lifetimes here to be 'activated'. This has been pre-orchestrated, along with the souls they would meet that would help elevate them into the purpose of self-evolution and therefore planetary evolution. They designed their lives in great detail to assist the greater good. They are the ones who naturally have a bigger-picture perspective and who are naturally able to see humanity as a whole.

Starseeds have specific missions to assist Planet Earth and her peoples to bring in the golden age. Suffering the same birth amnesia we all go through, starseed souls differ in that they are encoded with a 'wake-up call' designed to activate them at a pre-determined moment in life. Awakening can be gentle and gradual, or quite dramatic and abrupt. Either way, the soul amnesia starts to fall away so that they can consciously carry out their missions. Often, they are here to create new systems where old ones aren't working, like the mental health one, for instance (wink, wink). Their activations help them with their connection to their higher self so they can be largely guided by their inner knowing.

Many starseeds are practised in rapid spiritual growth, able to clear limiting patterns and fears that might take earth humans many lifetimes to accomplish. You may identify as one of these clearly because you are already aware of your own activation, or you may have been going through an awakening process that feels like life has become a jigsaw puzzle of psychic phenomena, where you are feeling like you are picking up clues from the universe but are not really able to fit it all together yet. This can feel like you are going crazy and are different to everyone around you. Without a reference point, you can fall into the trap of judging yourself as weird and crazy. Starseeds also suffer a lot of depression and anxiety, often with the feeling of wanting to go 'home'. The words channelled below are by the Pleiadians, served to awaken you further. Allow them to resonate within you to better serve you at this time.

The Pleiadians on Starseeds

There are those among you whose past lives have been predominately experienced in other lifeforms not of the human kind. You are human beings. A being is vibrational in nature and the vibrational part of you is heightened; this means that in your very nature you are sensitive to vibration, that being what you call emotion, or energy in motion. You know on a very deep level how to communicate telepathically, sense thought forms, emotional energy forms. This makes it easy for you to read others, sense people's motivations and sense their vibrations, which you may call getting a bad feeling about someone, or a good feeling. You naturally have highly tuned radar for truth and integrity, and falsehood is something you naturally repel. Your alignment to these things resides in your DNA. Your memory contains such experiences as teleportation, telekinesis and telepathy, and a lot of you are not used to being encased in a body, having lived lives in pure consciousness. This means that the feeling of being in a body resembles feelings of being trapped and confined. Language feels overrated and communication is difficult and tiresome. As a star being, 'work' and 'education' were more about experience and expansion of vibration rather than that of meaningless facts and having to earn anything, so opposition to education and work is strong within you and you may be labelled as lazy or oppositional to such constructs.

As an advanced soul who has lived lives in a community where all beings were enlightened and ascended (because you lived on a whole planet that had ascended), your being is not used to such things as conflict, only harmony, and general conflict within you and around you brings you great disharmony and soul pain as it is so foreign to your soul memory. Your affinity to freedom is second to none. You were once free to roam the multiverse and see and experience as you pleased, and you understood that there were many different species all from the same source, and judgement was not in your vocabulary since you did not even need a vocabulary to describe anything. Everything was felt, known and understood only at the vibrational level. Because you lived many lives not encased in a body, you have a natural ability to be outside of the human body. This may have caused you some mishap in this life, as being out of the body means you can travel into other realms and dimensions which this world teaches you are not real.

The disharmony that this creates is a source of great soul pain. Combined with the lack of knowledge of such information, confusion ensues. But here is the great thing; we are now entering a time of remembering. Your indigenous, those native to the lands of earth, have called your current era the Dreamtime, or the land of dreaming, but how the golden age is coming and how enlightenment and ascension is available to all is through the period and age of remembering. That time is upon us now. In your dualistic fields of earth, the veils of illusion are slowly lifting. For the law of polarity is creating a shift. There have been many predictions of a polar shift, but the polar shift that is to occur is within you. Where there has been darkness, the polar opposite is light; where there is confusion, the polar opposite is clarity; where there has been despair, the polar opposite is joy. How this is occurring is part of a great cycle which cannot be stopped, and it is occurring now at rapid speed. Just as the seasons cannot be stopped and just as the sun will always rise at the dawn of a new day, this shift is inevitable and is here. You do not need to do anything, except to go with it.

Keepers and Seekers – The Starseed Calling

Because of the planetary shifts occurring, starseeds are awakening in greater numbers as they were pre-destined to awaken themselves. Some have important tasks, and unless they really know the truth of these important feelings of a larger purpose, they could be construed as grandiose ideas. There is nothing grandiose about being of service to fellow mankind. There is nothing grandiose about imparting ancient knowledge that is within you to the masses. For some of you are seekers of truth and some of you are keepers. The seekers are looking for the keepers for the exchange; the exchange of ancient knowledge to be disseminated and used to bring harmony to this place. Some of you are deeply hurt by what you see – the wars, the violence, the judgement and pain. Your souls cry out for it to be the way you remember. The green you see is not the green you remember and as you try and make your way through the world the best way you know how, you cannot bury these feelings. When will it stop? This pain you feel inside. When will the planet stop dying, when will people wake up and see what's really going on, that you know deep inside and barely speak of, because 'they' don't seem to know what you sense and feel.

Sometimes, you want to violently shake them, and scream at them to wake up, but then you are suppressed by the fact that you yourself are still living like them, that you haven't found your own personal freedom. You see the pain, the bullshit that's going on, the control, the enslavement across all the systems, political, financial, educational and medical and yet you feel powerless, that somehow you are responsible for something big. You have the desire to shift these corrupt systems from the ground up if only you knew how, because something inside of you knows that they are rotten to the core. You want to find your place and you know that life is not meant to be about misery, so you gravitate towards excitement and adventure, all the things your soul loves to experience but somehow you forget you are still living in what feels like a wasteland, a forgotten land, and you sometimes see the irony that you have a memory of forgetting something but can't remember exactly what that 'something' is.

You feel a rising, a sense of rebellion, a stirring that you've tried to silence yet it won't stop. Like a snowball down a mountain collecting speed, the rising keeps coming, like relentless waves that keep lapping onto the shore, the stirring prods at you to pay attention. You swear that sometimes you can actually hear the words, 'Wake up. Wake up'.

Divine Intervention

De-Vine ... The fact that you all derive from a long vine, a lineage of light, and when you are in your divinity you practise not being of this world, but being in it. Detach from the drama around you, especially the one within that loves drama, the ego. To be in touch with your divinity is to hold great wisdom and love for yourself and your journey. You are travellers through a great series of ages, growing and maturing as you go. The importance of knowing your heritage that is not from earth is to be able to work with and call upon higher energies that can assist from higher realms. Einstein once said, "We cannot solve our problems with the same thinking we used when we created them". To really attain great wisdom beyond even Einstein himself, is by obtaining it away from the polluted energies of the earth. If you're not seeing the wisdom in what we are telling you, let us explain it like this: Einstein developed amazing theories, some of which could have brought great peace and harmony, but your world used its knowledge for destruction. Even in this you can see that knowledge, when taken into the wrong hands, can be used destructively. Who used this knowledge destructively? Your enslavers, the ones who are keeping all control with all the knowledge they have. They have been using it to enslave you and they wish to disconnect you from your true heritage so that you do not have the knowledge that they have, for it would then be an even playing field. They have known about this golden age coming; the prophecies have not been able to be suppressed, maybe manipulated and misunderstood but the new age, the golden age, is something that cannot be stopped.

This is where divine intervention comes in. Although you live in a free-will universe, the knowledge of this has been hidden and so we are here to assist you to understand how you can claim your divine right to divine intervention. Perhaps we can explain it like this. In communities and families where there are elders, one may go and consult to get a higher perspective because of their 'age-old wisdom', yes? Well, what about being able to consult with age-old wisdom from not only enlightened beings but ascended beings who can assist you from their wisdom of having walked the path you are walking now, who know all the truth, the whole truth and nothing but the truth? Sounds great, right? Some of you already know how to do this, but the perception is that this truth is only reserved for the gifted, or it is delving into dark forces, witchery, blasphemous, dangerous. Do you see all the ways you have been blocked?

Divine intervention is real, and when you ask for assistance it is heard. Many of you now work with the 'universe'. Universe, give me this, you say. Provide me with abundance. The universe is you! You are the stars that make up the universe. The stars of this stage-play called life. When you ask the universe for something you are indeed calling upon yourself to rise up to what is needed to provide it for yourself. Yes, there are other beings such as us to call upon, but we are here to only guide you, help you remember your true divinity. You are special, you are loved and you are supported by those who have walked a similar path, both in your earthly ancestry line and in your star ancestry. As above, so below. Same same but different.

Armed with the Key of Divinity, it's time to obtain the Key of Ascension.

The Key of Ascension

We descended from mastery and we are on the return journey home. All there is to do is to remember.

Me

The Galactic Federation of Light

I am in a dream-like state. I am practising with eyes wide open. Then, out of nowhere, like a flash in my brain, I have a memory. I am at a round table. I am one of 12. There are 11 other beings present. We are not human and I am aware that I am present at a galactic federation council meeting. I am in the presence of very wise beings with a significant role in the galaxy. We are discussing the fate of the earth and its inhabitants. There is talk of interventions to assist humanity so that they don't destroy their planet and the entire human race. Strategies are being discussed and solutions being proposed. There is a pause in discussion.

"I want to volunteer".

I am met with surprised looks. "I'll go down. We need some of us down there on ground level to help out."

"You know that isn't necessary," one board member says. "You know it's much easier to work from here at this level; there are other intervention strategies."

"But I want to; this is important," I reply, feeling insistent.

"You know how dangerous it is. You'll have to go through the veil of forgetfulness," another member says with eyebrows raised. "You know we've lost quite a few through the birth portal, just as eager as you! They're lost now. Forgotten completely who they are, trapped in the karmic cycles."

"But I know I can do it! I'll program myself to remember! I'll select a time in my timeline to remember this very moment to awaken me. I know I can do it. A lot can be done from the ground," I say, somewhat ambitiously.

"Okay, well, you don't need to convince us. The choice is yours."

"It's done then! I'm going down! I'll keep in touch when I remember, okay?"

Woah! Out of this world, right? Like, literally. I mean, who has experiences like that unless they are hypnotised or in a past-life regression? I sat with this memory for quite some time, wondering if what I remembered should stay between me and my journal. I wondered if there were others out there like me who felt crazy, with an unknown sense of importance in their cellular memory. I had this memory before I was out of the ET closet. I had come out of the closet as a psychic, but every time I had made mention of ETs, I usually got a weird look or the conversation was hijacked by someone and directed to a new topic to avoid being uncomfortable. These days, I obviously don't really care anymore. I'd rather be called crazy than be pushing down all that I feel, remember and know within me. And besides, depressing my truth within always led to depression.

Funny that! The word depression means to push something down. I always get led to confirmation, though, and although it was years later, I stumbled upon *The Three Waves of Volunteers* by Dolores Cannon and *Destiny of Souls* by Michael Newton, two books that are filled with transcribed conversations with their clients from past-life regression and hypnotherapy sessions, similar to this memory I had.

Ascension

The planet, according to many great prophecies, is going through a collective awakening – an ascension process. This is indeed an exciting time. Ascension energies create sudden streams of consciousness, sudden awareness of signs and synchronicities, and an undeniable hunch that there is something greater going on; a feeling that the coincidences are maybe not just coincidences, but evidence of a great intelligence, some cosmic design that is supporting something to rise from within. However, not understood, it could make those who are unaware believe that they are either physically or mentally ill.

In very simple terms, to ascend means to rise. We all descended here – otherwise known as the great fall – and ascension just means we are now rising again. Contrary to what is taught in some religions, it is important to know that ascension is not reserved for holy men, but is available to every one of us. Ascension is the process of increasing in frequency. It happens as you bring more of your divine light and presence into physical form. As a part of the ascension process, your aura expands, your chakras open and evolve, and dormant DNA becomes activated. Progress on your ascension path allows you to experience the higher vibrational realms of multi-dimensional consciousness.

It is one thing to become enlightened, and another to ascend. The difference is that you need to firstly become light in order to rise.

Enlightenment leads to ascension. Ascension means you are no longer stuck in the karmic cycle of having to repeatedly return to earth. There is great assistance being made by those races outside the earth system to help humanity to ascend by a whole range of light codes being filtered through. These are known as ascension downloads, and they filter through the dense and darker matrix energies to liberate humans into truth and light.

Increased spiritual perception, awakened psychic and spiritual abilities, awakened compassion for humanity, the earth and all beings, and a greater alignment with divine synchronicity are all symptoms of ascension. There are, however, some ascension symptoms that can cause real discomfort. Challenges, emotional struggles, and mental and physical pain may occur as you walk the ascension path of transforming dense and lower vibrations into a high-vibrational crystalline light form. It's like a recalibration that isn't always comfortable, as your light body is being formed on the cellular level.

Ascension is an alchemical process that is experienced on every level of mind, body, and spirit. When you are on an ascension path, any area of your life in which you are still engaged in the old paradigm, or dense energy, comes up for review in some way. Things that no longer serve your highest and greatest good will crumble, fall away and dissolve to make way for what will ultimately serve you in the highest possible vibration for your life. Relationships, jobs, hobbies, habits, beliefs, living arrangements, diet, patterns, belief systems and more may change, fall away, or be transformed into a higher vibrational manifestation that more fully serves your soul growth and ascension path.

Let go or be pushed. This may sound harsh or unfair, but ascension is an unstoppable and inevitable force, and if we can accept it, the shift can be graceful, or if we refuse to let go and hang on to old ways of being, then shit is going to get difficult. The universe is basically saying that fighting it will only make it worse. Some ascension symptoms are listed below. It's important to listen to your body at these times and honour it. Extra sleep might be needed, or less food. You might feel crazy and/or tempted to seek medicines to alleviate these symptoms, but know that all physical symptoms are energetic in nature. Treating your symptoms with self-love and natural remedies where possible is best for integration.

ASCENSION SYMPTOMS

◊   Headaches

◊   Digestion issues

◊   Earaches and ears ringing

◊   Deeper senses and more occurrences of déjà vu

◊   Feeling that you know others when you haven't met them before (soul memory activation)

◊   Nausea and dizziness

◊   Sleeplessness

◊   Extreme tiredness, lethargy

◊   Feelings of dissociation (being out of the body).

From 3D to 5D

For a whole planet to ascend, all its inhabitants must also complete their own personal ascensions. We are going through a great shift from third-dimension consciousness to the fifth-dimensional. To put it simply, the third dimension is where the human ego resides, and the fifth is where unconditional love for all beings lives. The third dimension is self-centred, and the fifth is service-centred. It is a way of going from living from the head to living from the heart. It is not an easy transition because all the darkness within is rising to the surface to be cleared. You will be drawn into situations and experiences and will meet people (from your soul family) who will assist this process of purging. All lower aspects of the personality – old hurts, resentments, patterns of behaviour that are of lower vibration – are on the list to go! The transition can be painful, as we are called to let go of old comfortable ways of being that don't serve the new collective of unconditional love. Some of this letting go can cause depression, anxiety and feelings of dissociation. This transition has never occurred on Planet Earth before and is necessary for its survival. Look at where our self-seeking ways have got us as a collective. Destroying each other and our planet! This ascension process is being well guided by those who have achieved personal ascension by the ascended masters, as well as those who have achieved planetary ascension in the galactic realms.

Ascended Masters

Ascended masters are spiritually enlightened beings who, in past lives, were ordinary humans but have undergone a series of spiritual transformations and passed the test of challenging initiation processes. They expanded their soul's growth enough to transcend all their karma and leave the karmic cycle to ascend to a higher realm. St Germain, Metatron, Hathor, and El Morya are examples, amongst many others. They are often regarded as saints of their time who dedicated their lives to the service and liberation of others. Metatron, for example, was known as Enoch, an ancestor of Noah who was said to have walked with God. They are believed to have transcended the human ego and become one with the mind of God/Universe in human form, something which normally happens after death.

According to the Ascended Master Teachings, a 'master', 'shaman' or 'spiritual master' is a human being who has taken the Fifth Initiation and is thereby capable of dwelling on the fifth dimension. It has been predicted by the Ashtar Command that those who ascended earth in the first wave will be given the opportunity to return in the ascended state, to awaken the rest of humanity to show and teach others of the ascension opportunity. In the Book of Enoch and amongst ancient Native American prophecies, as well as in the book of Revelation in the Bible, there is mention of a sudden appearance of 144,000 ascended masters on the earth, who will transform the world and push back the clouds of darkness and close the gap between heaven and earth.

In the book of Revelation, it is said that these 144,000 would have been cleansed by the time of great distress, a seven-year period of great tribulation. Perhaps it was a series of hardships and initiations so that they were truly ready to lead the way forward for the rest of humanity. It has been said that these masters will create a wave whereby more will be affected until everyone is affected in the group ascension process, and this wave will work to transform humanity by creating a tipping point where everyone else will have no choice but to slide into their own awakenings, whether they are seeking it or not, under the majority rules effect.

Do not allow your mind to tell you that your sense of importance or feeling that you are on a mission are symptoms of a sickness. They are grandiose thoughts, yes, grounded in a deep, ancient truth rather than a die-gnosis! Same same but different. Remember how important you are, that you are playing a vital role in the expansion of everyone's consciousness and pathway to ascension. What you do and how you live affects the fate of this world. You can't get more important than that!

Marie ANTOINETTE

The Pleiadian View on Ascension

What is ascension and why is it important?

Ascension relates to a rising; a rising of one's consciousness to encompass all truth, all love and all light. It is a marriage of the higher realms, a graduation, if you will, into higher realms. It is liberation of being completely out of the lower self (ego) into the higher state of the higher self. In religious texts throughout history, ascension has been referred to those who have died and ascended into heaven. But there is a bridge that has been built, a bridge between heaven and earth. The veil between these two worlds has been collapsing, and the collapse of this veil will be the merge so that heaven can operate here in this time, on this earth. Often it is referred to as the golden age. On a personal level, this means that it will be possible for ascension to occur in your human bodies without leaving your body, into what is referred to as death. Some call this the fifth dimension. It is the same same but different.

How does one live being in this heavenly state? What does living in the higher self-state look like? It means that you are aware of your existence as a spiritual being in a human body; a soul with great wisdom and knowledge located within your cellular structure, a knowing that there is no disease within you, only outside of you. Everyone around you is experiencing this life through their own lens and you are all one, aspects of the whole divine intelligence. Everything is reflected to you and through you. Your experience is directly created by you and life is not happening to you.

The many truths that reside within you are, however, in direct opposition to almost everything you know and have been taught. This is the real disease and malady. The malady of confusion. What is right and what is real. This is for you to navigate on your path to ascension, but know this: it is possible to know all truth about the nature of the multiverse. You are a part of it, which means the truth is

106

within you. What distracts you is your conditioning, your beliefs and your environment. You live in a world of distortion, illusion and lies. Ascension into the higher self will help you realise the powerful and magnificent being that you really are. That what you perceive and believe is ultimately your reality. That the fabric of your world has been hidden in mistruths but the reality lies in cosmic consciousness and is based in science. Not the science that has been falsely perpetuated upon you through false studies and random trials, but the very fabric of quantum physics and mechanics.

The real truth lies in science, not religion. Religious sects declared war on science many years ago, and still to this day, religion has been used to divide people through the ages and is responsible for many wars that have been waged. Religion does not come from the source of creation. The biggest saviour for all of you is YOU. Again, we tell you, the truth is inside of you, in your very cells. De-program yourself from global fear, community fear and personal fears, and this will begin your liberation from the ego self. This is first and foremost the path that is needed to begin the journey to enlightenment and ascension. Are enlightenment and ascension two different things? We say this: Enlightenment is the journey towards ascension. First, you must bring light to all the darkness within you. You must be vibrating at a higher rate to rise, to ascend, as it were. This is not about being holy, as what you may have been taught in religious matters, but one of weight and density. For something to rise, it must be light and not heavy. What is keeping you down are things such as fear, anger, revenge, resentment, pity, remorse, guilt and shame. Your transformation to bring you to the path of enlightenment is to replace these with love, joy, compassion, understanding, forgiveness, acceptance, gratitude, grace, excitement.

When your vibration is raised, your soul comes alive and self-seeking slips away; this is where service-oriented thinking occurs and divine soul missions are birthed. 'How can I help my fellow travellers' becomes the thought of the day. How can I use my experiences so far to benefit others? You see, self-liberation enables us to liberate others. Not

107

because we are somehow healed and perfect in nature, and therefore can lead others – these thoughts are based in ego. Everyone is their own leader; a true leader fosters the leader within, by the power of example, wisdom and encouragement.

What is planetary ascension and how does it affect personal ascension?

For you to understand planetary ascension, you must first understand personal ascension in a bit more depth. Personal ascension is a process by which all light, all love and all truth is restored to you. This is what it is referred to as the monad or the law of one, a returning through from whence you came. There is great irony in your spiritual circles when people speak of being on a journey, as most do not fully understand the fact that indeed you are. You have left home, where source creation is, and your journey is to experience that which you planned and then return home.

Can you see how so many of you end up lost? Some of you have forgotten, some have remembered and yet are still distracted, and some of you remember everything but are using this knowledge to suppress and control others. Ascension therefore is not a process whereby you gather information, learn from others and develop new skills, but rather a deep remembering and awakening and then a calling to action for what is needed within you to awaken others. For it is in remembering we must forget, and in forgetting we must remember. This is the great spiritual teaching that is splintered across all religions that comes from the monad; to share what is within you. It is not about preaching, but rather, shining your light for others so that it acts like a beacon and assists to light the way for others.

If you can, imagine that you are all ships at sea and there is great conflict and turmoil where there is no lighthouse to light the way. But here is the great myth that has been perpetuated amongst you through the corruption of religions. This myth seeks you to believe that the light must be shone by a leader, a select few who know how to light the way and all knowledge and truth is reserved only for the holy and those who are chosen. May these words printed here serve to remind you that you are already chosen. YOU chose you to have your experience, to start your journey. There isn't anything to earn your way into what is depicted as heaven; you just need to remember the way you came so you can go home. Remember the story of Hansel and Gretel, who ensured they knew their way home by leaving a trail? You have also left a trail that, as you awaken, you will discover. Like a giant jigsaw puzzle, you will gather the pieces and see the whole picture.

This is why the Christian religion and other religions have been so corrupted, because there are great teachings within that are designed to help us remember and be the light and example for us, but so many of you have turned your backs on these belief systems because you sense the corruption. In a way, this is a glorious thing to occur, because you must then seek further, seek deeper within yourselves to find a deeper point of reference for truth. This is where your senses shall awaken, your intuition will rise and you will intuitively know how to deal with situations without the voice of conditioning coming in to steal its wisdom.

The embracing of your intuition is pivotal to your development and relationship with the self, separate to the lower ego mind and the conditioned myths you have been living by. Real truth and authenticity will come from within you and flow like an eternal spring. Mastering of the intuition, your sixth sense, will enable you to come to all of your senses, including your seventh one! And as you come to your senses, you will see that the world you live in doesn't make sense, and that you were not unwell at all. It is the world you have been living in, with all its untruths and myths, that has been keeping you away from personal relief and success and happiness. With this will come empathy for self that propels you forward into a path of self-understanding, compassion and unconditional love. An unconditional love that your soul remembers from source, and that, dear ones, is the key to finding your path home. This is why all great leaders and teachers speak of love for thyself. Unconditional love for self is paramount. However, whilst you are in the confines of a mental health system which seeks to encourage you to see yourself as sick and one-sided, you will always see yourselves at fault. The charade is up. There is no-thing wrong with you, only the absence of truth and the vibrational alignment between you and unconditional love.

Take that in; breathe that into every cell of your being.

Planetary Ascension

NOW, let's talk about planetary ascension.

Here's the good news: your personal ascension is already guaranteed. Yes, that's correct. This is because of the collective consciousness that exists. ALL living things come from source creation, even those that you believe may not come from light, and everything must return at some point as it is divine law which cannot be stopped. Right now in human evolution, the entire planet you live on is in its return journey to source. Imagine, if you will, a great cycle. Cycles are inevitable, are they not? They just are, they just exist and they cannot be stopped unless the cycle is complete. There are many divine laws that you may not understand, and these laws operate to rule the cosmos and the greater order of things in the multiverse. Just as you understand the cycle of your sun rising and falling, etc., there are greater cycles that relate to your planet.

The majority of you do not understand these cycles because the information has been kept from you. There may be more of an opportunity for us in other writings to discuss some of these cycles and the agendas behind their lack of disclosure, but for now and for the purpose of demonstrating planetary ascension, we would say that what affects one affects the whole. Because you are connected to each and every person living on this planet at this time, you are then equally *and proportionately affected. This means that as one awakens, the other is affected. You would have heard the saying, 'you are who you hang around', and this is true for all living in community.*

It is co-created energies that many of you do not understand and the secrets of how creation occurs, some of which we can share with you, that will help you to understand that everything is affected by the other. Nothing is alone in the universe, especially YOU! It has already been prophesied by many, including the current channel, that when enough of the human race is awake, there will be a flow-on effect, a quickening like a snowball will occur where personal and planetary ascension is inevitable. This means that spontaneous awakenings will occur where there has been no part to play of the individual. That by no action on their part, and by pure energetic osmosis, people will begin to experience the shift. A CALLING WITHIN TO RISE, LIKE A CLARION CALL, AND THE CALL WILL BE HEARD FROM WITHIN EN MASSE. Your ancient cultures have prophesied this. 2012 was the first wave, the ending of the great cycle of destruction, and the return journey began.

Many of you experienced sudden bursts of insight, sudden skills of prophecy, telepathy and psychic ability. Many of you, depending on where you were at in your life, experienced this well, and welcomed these new skills with surprise but were able to integrate these with the support around you. Many of you decided at this time to leave jobs or relationships in search of something new, even when you didn't know what that something new was.

Others struggled, not having had these experiences before, and with no-one around you to help you integrate such experiences, went into states of spiritual emergency, unable to integrate these, and a lot of you ended up feeling crazy, disconnected and at a loss for words to understand what you experienced. And yet a lot of you felt nothing significant had changed, and all this talk about the end of some world as we know it was ludicrous and were missing the deeper meaning.

But know this; as this great shift has already occurred and nothing can stop its ascension, depending on where you are at in your journey, the ascension will continue. Again everything is affected and a calibration of energy is needed on a personal level for the changes of the planet to be integrated personally.

Armed with the Key of Ascension, it's time to obtain the Key of Truth.

The Key of Truth

**Find the truth and the truth shall set you free,
but not before it pisses you off first.**

Unknown

The world – let's face it – is filled with lies and bullshit; filled with smoke and mirrors. It's no wonder many of us are walking around in a daze, trying to decipher fact from fiction. Unfortunately, the real truth is often painful. Not only the truth about ourselves, but the real truth about our world. To find the real truth about the many mysteries of our world, we first need to understand and discover the real truth within. On our journey towards enlightenment and ascension, it's important to clear out our internal houses. Mental health issues are often based in what's real, what is not, what is true and what is false on all levels. This is why truth liberates us. Clarity appears where confusion once lived and our soul is renewed because truth is in alignment with who we are.

When we live in integrity and truth, all is well; there is peace and harmony. When there is dishonesty, information left out, manipulation and intentional deceit, it harms our very nature as infinite multi-dimensional souls having human experiences, because truth is the language of the soul. The soul is truth's keeper. Therefore, we seek truth so frantically because we are seeking equilibrium.

How many times do you lie to others to 'protect' them? Dishonesty is deeply embedded in our society and psyches to such a degree it has become 'normal'. It's almost ironic that one of the symptoms of a mental illness classified as Asperger's is the overwhelming compulsion to tell the truth all the time. Seen as a lack of social graces, it makes everyone uncomfortable. Those of you who are outspoken and can't help yourselves could easily be on the autism spectrum! Dishonesty is generational. We learn to lie from our parents.

Here's a common scenario: If a child walks into a room where their parents have been arguing, usually the parents will be quiet because they have the belief that it's not okay to argue in front of their children. The child feels the uncomfortable energy in the air even though they are not saying a word, and might then ask the parents what's wrong. And the usual response is 'nothing'. This is where it all begins. The denial of intuition. The child realises that they've had a feeling and a sense of knowing, but because the adults around them are telling them that there is nothing wrong, they start to trust their head instead of their heart. This plays out a lot through many experiences until we end up losing ourselves and not being able to make sense of our emotions as adults, and we lose our connection to our intuition and gut feelings.

I'm sure you remember other lies, perhaps told to you by your parents who decided through an illusion of wisdom that it was better for you not to know something. We lie to protect others' feelings and we lie to protect our own through the false belief that we are responsible for other people's feelings and vice versa. This creates an ongoing cognitive dissonance, i.e. a disconnection from the heart's truth to the lie held in the head, which is at the heart of all human suffering on many levels. Ongoing cognitive dissonance contributes to feelings of confusion, depression and anxiety. By getting conflicting messages, we create chaos in our minds and we start fighting with ourselves, and so the only solution to avoid 'doing your head in' is to connect to your heart and find the truth that will set you free.

Truth with Self and Others

Spirituality is not about being nice and polite; it's about telling the truth.

Me

The capacity for you to be honest with others can only be measured by the capacity you have to be honest with yourself. You may hide from the truth because of toxic shame; you withhold the truth, believing that withholding is not lying and not understanding that this too is a form of dishonesty.

We have become a society where a lot of us are merely co-existing or cohabitating rather than being in deep and meaningful connection with each other. Deep feelings of disconnection to the world and others under the guise of depression are often the empathic response to a world that your soul knows is not operating in truth. And forget about bullshitting yourself about your own truth, especially if you're a sensitive type. You're only going to find yourself confused and in great internal pain until you can face yourself with an open heart. I have often run from seeing the truth about myself that was operating in the world due to toxic shame. I saw lies, selfishness and self-centredness, and the world was a cold, hostile one for quite some time until I faced up to and shifted those very things within me. The truth was and always will be that what we see in the world is merely a reflection of what is operating in us.

Projection

"If what you seek is Truth, there is one thing
you must have above all else."

"I know. An overwhelming passion for it."

"No. An unremitting readiness to admit you may be wrong."

Anthony de Mello

The unhealed parts of us often create a distortion that the world and connection with others is painful. The way in which our woundedness bleeds out and taints our relationships is through the creative adjustment, or artful way of projection. As humans with a heightened pleasure centre in our brain, we are more inclined to do absolutely anything to avoid pain. It's a deeply primal self-preservation thing we do to protect ourselves. What we cannot face within ourselves or what is repressed out of our conscious mind is seen in another. The universe and those we co-habit it with are all essentially mirrors, mirroring back to us that which is unseen in us. We may, for example, perceive people in our lives as selfish or needy when these are the disowned parts that are operating in us.

How many times do you reach out to others, wanting them to provide you with the love you need, only to fall short? Those with abuse and trauma in their histories seek more wildly through desperation what their souls know and understand they deserve. Entitlement, neediness and expectations are the causes of most disharmony in relationships and come from the core wounding that needs to be expressed and released. Then, the journey of providing to ourselves that which we never received provides the pathway to self-harmony.

Loving in order to be loved is futile. It comes from a place of lack and need. You need to be in love with yourself, and with your life.

116

This doesn't mean waiting or striving to get the things you want in your life, but a way of unconditional love no matter where you are at in life. Where there is inner harmony, love can thrive. That harmony must come from within by finding the union within yourself through your mind and heart and giving your soul the things that you expect from others in the form of love, attention, dedication and affection.

In my journey, I have had to release all the pain of not receiving the love my soul knew it deserved, and feel and release the wounds of abandonment. I am a work in progress and still healing and releasing many deep layers because my soul, in its wisdom, chose to be on this path of this return journey to unconditional love via ways of experience, predominantly in one lifetime. A lot of you have also chosen this path. What is not broken cannot be healed. What is not lost cannot be found. What is not incomplete cannot be transformed. My close relationship with the divine has not made me impervious to life's lessons and they cannot stop me acting out from a wounded space, but they certainly make the path much easier when I listen and act on the wisdom. However, wisdom is obsolete without surrender. A hardened heart with its layers of protection built around it can only be healed with the soft, forgiving, nurturing side in all of us, despite our gender.

There are no shortcuts to wellness. The shortcuts you attempt only serve to lengthen the process of healing. The woundedness of what you felt as a child, in all the ways you didn't receive the love that you needed, doesn't go away simply because you grow up and get a job, a career and get married. It stays there in your consciousness, in your cellular memory, and when something or someone 'out there' pushes the wounds, you avoid that something or someone and move on, missing the lesson and opportunity to heal the wound. Your soul draws you to these experiences to heal itself; you miss the soul's memo on this, and go on and re-experience the wounding somewhere else, with someone else and cry, "why me?"

Ironically, as a child, when you are given less than what you need emotionally, you blame yourself with a personal self-statement of "I'm not good enough", and as an adult when others fall short of your expectations, the core wounding of not feeling good enough is projected out as you blame others, essentially with the same unconscious reflected statement of "you're not good enough". You may lie and manipulate in order to get what you want, just like a child operating from this core wounding, exerting power over others instead of coming from a place of personal power.

Personal Power

**It is no measure of health to be well adjusted
to a profoundly sick society.**

Jiddu Krishnamurti

Blame and victimhood are two of the biggest neuroses in our society. It is deeply embedded, and we learn to blame and be victims from our parents, teachers and friends. We hear things like, "he pissed me off, he made me feel upset, he dumped me and ruined my life, he did this to me, she did that to me". True power is knowing that nobody can do anything to you at any moment or any time. You choose your experience, you choose your reaction, you choose your responses, and you are in charge of the energy in motion in your own body and in your energy field. Just think about that for a moment.

Think about the power that that brings to you, knowing that you do not have to respond in any way, shape or form other than the way in which you would like to. It's a mental and emotional discipline, yes, but it will bring you equilibrium in your life like nothing else.

What are seen as symptoms of mental disorders often stem from emotional and energetic imbalances in the body. The energy centres connected to personal power in our bodies are the solar plexus and sacral chakras. The solar plexus, when balanced, has you taking responsibility for your life, taking control, having confidence in forming personal opinions and beliefs, having clarity of judgement, personal identity, self-assurance, self-discipline and self-confidence. Notice the string of 'self' in this statement. Your solar plexus is your focal point of the relationship you have with yourself. However, for you to be able to create what you want in life, the sacral energy chakra must also be clear for the solar plexus to be working in conjunction.

The sacral chakra is also about the self and its relationship with the other. 'Sacral' is taken from the Sanskrit word *svadhisthana*, meaning 'dwelling place of the self'. This chakra is associated with emotions, feelings, relating and relationships, expression of sexuality, sensual pleasure, creativity and feeling of the outer and inner worlds. It's particularly active in our sexuality and the expression of our sensual and sexual desires.

Motivated by pleasure, the sacral chakra is the driving force for the enjoyment of life through the senses. When it is closed or out of balance it causes depression, poor boundaries, being overly sensitive, indulgent or aggressive; it induces us into a state of fear and/or anxiety along with panic attacks, and causes us to be manipulative and behave in co-dependent ways.

Besides developing a relationship with yourself via therapy, reflective journaling and meditation, these chakra points can be healed through energetic healing practices and guided visualisations. The other way, in relation to the mind, is to look at your beliefs and shift the ones that don't support you.

Beliefs

Until you make the unconscious conscious, it will direct your life and you will call it fate.

Carl Jung

Bruce Lipton is a pioneer on belief systems. He wrote a book called *The Biology of Belief,* and in it he describes the scientific approach to our belief systems and how they create our reality. What we be-live becomes true. Our beliefs are like computer programs running through us, and they are programs from our unconscious programming that then create our reality. Our beliefs direct our experience, reactions and help us make meaning of things in life. It is the beliefs held in the subconscious mind that are really running the show.

What is reality? Mental illness symptoms confine us into one form of reality, but reality is actually very personal. Our personal realities are created by us. They are formed through our thoughts, our beliefs and our experiences. It's quite interesting that we allow one person or a medically trained professional to tell us what is normal for us in our reality. Lack of boundaries is also an unhealthy social construct embedded in the collective consciousness that allows beliefs and ideas to be imposed on us. We allow ourselves to be subliminally informed about what to believe; from religion and faith to what we should feel and think, not to mention the ongoing suppression of whether ETs exist or not!

We are all sovereign beings who have the power to choose our own reality. This is what I teach in my programs and why doing basic psychic future readings is not so much my forte anymore. Although I have the ability to see the future, when people come to me for a future reading and ask, "What's in store for me in my future?" I feel like saying, "Well, whatever you want it to be". I once did a reading with someone where I had to tell her that there were no changes in her future. I couldn't actually see any developments. I told her that the only thing I could see was her going to work in her job, where she was extremely unhappy, coming home, isolating herself, watching a bit of TV, having dinner and then going to bed, feeling depressed.

The woman was shocked that I could see her daily grind of a life so clearly. It was the hard, blunt truth, because she was obviously in a rut. She had come to see me to perhaps get some hope that better things were on the horizon. Essentially, I had to be the bearer of bad news in telling her that there was nothing in her future that was going to bring her happiness. Rather than just having a simple reading, I asked her, "Would you like to learn how to create something else in your life? Because for it to change, you will need to change the beliefs that are creating your current reality." She was open to this idea and I did an energetic clearing, particularly on her sacral and solar plexus and helped her shift some of her unconscious beliefs. She felt amazing, and to demonstrate my point we did another future reading, except this time, what was revealed was that a change in employment was coming, along with a new relationship!

The Biggest Illusion of All

I've found that if I want some magnificent 'out of this world' advice, I've got to go out of this world to get it.

Me

When it comes to holistic health, it is important to know the truth of all realities. We can be affected by other realms that can affect us positively but also destabilise us. Many ancient and eastern tradition-based cultures understand this, but in the western world the truth has been majorly suppressed and depleted of all truth and integrity.

Nothing dies, it just changes form. I wish someone had taught me that when I was a kid. I grew up feeling puzzled and lied to about being told that nothing existed after death. It made no sense to me. I was fascinated with death in a way I never dared to tell anyone about. When I was older I just assumed it was part of depression. But then I found a poem I had written as a teenager about wanting to go to the other side and tell people of the place I'd been. Without realising, I was expressing my desire to be a psychic medium!

The drawing towards death isn't always about wanting to die, but a felt memory of where you've just been as a soul. There is little known about the soul in many cultures, and if you've been raised to believe that this is the only life we live, there was nothing before and there will be nothing after, then the soul is already in conflict because it knows otherwise. The drawing towards death is, therefore, sometimes merely a soul curiosity, but because of how death is treated in western society, our minds can turn to something morbid or a desire to die. Death is representative of an ending of one cycle to the next and of rebirth.

Often our beliefs are tied to religion and faith. There's a joke in psychiatry that if you talk to God it's called praying, but if God talks back to you, then it's insanity. There's another saying that the first sign of madness is when you are talking to yourself. Where did these sayings come from? Do they support us in any way? These spiritual concepts are seen as madness in the mental health system.

My belief is that people suffering from mental illness hold keys of truth within them that differ from society's truth, which causes them a lot of pain. I don't believe that truth can be found in one single religion or one single belief, but there are truths in many that, when we string them together, are all the same same but different.

The Pleiadians on Truth

Well, what do you know? Only what you have been taught. Only what has been fed to you through the corridors of time and generations according to the earth field and grid. If you are seeking the truth outside of you, you will only get what is here on the planet, and how is that going for you all? Have you been able to eradicate world hunger? How is the poverty going? Are people still killing each other in the name of religion? Are the masses so traumatised on a cellular level that they have compartmentalised themselves in their minds to believe that all is well? It could be all well in your current reality, the one that you have created for yourself in your mind. However, there is a truth that resides in you that knows different. It is the truth in your being part of your humanness. It knows you are lying to yourself. It knows that you are connected to your people as one race and not separate countries and cultures, and it bleeds. It bleeds internally for the disconnection, the mass massacre, but the mind – the mind is clever. It is a self-regulating healing organism and in order to preserve and protect itself, it disassociated you from this truth. It is wisdom in action, for how would you live while your heart is bleeding? How would you continue to support yourself and others if you felt the depths of despair of what is happening, and so it disconnects you to protect you.

This is where the saying "you can't handle the truth" and cognitive dissonance come into play. You hide from the deepest truth that resides in you in order to cope and you disconnect from feeling that deep intrapsychic pain. Numbing yourself with the many things on offer to numb yourself with, you name it, anywhere and everywhere there are numbing agents to assist you, sometimes consciously, but mostly unconsciously.

In order to have good judgement, good discernment, one must reconnect. Connect back into the feeling zone so you can feel the vibe. You know, those vibrations of energy that you call 'good vibe' or 'bad vibe'. These vibes you get defy logical reasoning. A lot of you have lost the 'vibe'. You are vibrational beings first, human second. You are NOT human beings having a spiritual experience; you are multi-dimensional souls having a human experience. Same same but different!

Most of you are starting to realise more and more just how much deceit is in this world, and just how much you have been misled to believe certain things. We shall give you the example of the food pyramid. Most of you now know that if you invert that, it's closer to the real truth of better health and longevity. There are more and more articles on your internet starting with, "Everything they've ever told you about … is wrong".

And well done that people are sharing this information freely to assist others. Truth can appear as truth but be filled with lies. Imposters, spies and trickery live amongst you more than you currently know as a collective. For everything you think you know about the world you live in, there are 50,000 things you don't know. That's a ball-park figure of how much you've been kept in the dark and, make no mistake, the way you have been kept in the dark is no mistake. Do not fall into the trap of "we didn't know this", and "what we now know is …" with these latest discoveries. Advanced information on the human race, how the brain, body, spirit and soul works has been maintained in secret societies since the beginning.

The societies were kept secret because knowledge is power and some of this knowledge falling into the wrong hands could prove disastrous and destroy the world. Doesn't this all sound familiar? It's a theme amongst thousands of cartoons, films and sci-fi sectors, as well as supposed fairy tales such as Harry Potter. The very truth is sold to you as entertainment, as fiction! You see this good versus evil; this war that is going on is deeply embedded in your psyche. It's retained in your consciousness and we are here to tell you it is based more in truth than myth.

Just as you would invert your food pyramid for optimal health, you must invert and reverse everything else to see the true nature of the world and what is breeding truth and integrity.

Your symbols of various religious and mystery schools have been polluted and used against you. Many ancient symbols emanating virtues of sacredness, peace, and based in the light have been perverted, so that their use is one converted to dark energy. The pentagram, for example, is a beautiful symbol of spirit over matter and of the ascent of human to heaven, but when used upside-down it becomes a symbol of the dark forces used extensively in black magic.

The reality of the nonphysical realms have been kept from you under the guise of "what you don't know CAN harm you". Those who see themselves as light workers, who wish to believe that evil doesn't exist, are fooling themselves, because they find it more emotionally convenient to believe that light and protection works and faith is the best option; if you believe in a higher force such as God, you will be okay.

However, we tell you that this is an ignorant approach. There is a saying, "keep your friends close but your enemies closer". Your enemies have been hidden from you for good reason. If you don't know they exist and how they are working against you, you cannot do anything to stop them and remain blind. You can even be used in such a way that you are totally unaware, that you are even a prisoner and captive in anything.

We will be very clear. There is evil, but no hell. Hell is a state of being, not a place, just as heaven is. These places are in consciousness. There are light beings who work for the good of all and the collective across several different realms and dimensions. People can be haunted just as houses are. Madness is produced by believing that the haunting isn't real and is a figment of the imagination. For when truth is denied, confusion starts, confused thinking, distorted ...

sound familiar? These are the very symptoms of psychosis. Your western world believes that these are not real, but the ancient ones of this earth have known for many eons just what has been going on. Now do you see? Now do you understand why the indigenous have been hunted down in cold blood, segregated, customs and traditions destroyed and stolen, and the families brutally traumatised? The ones who collectively orchestrated such barbaric atrocities against a wise and gentle people did so with full knowledge of a seek-and-destroy campaign.

Trauma destroys memory. It keeps information fragmented and tortures on the soul level so that the soul cannot heal and pass through the after-world levels to choose in wisdom its next course of action. Instead, the soul gets stuck in suspension. We pause here to give you a breather. This is a lot to take in, is it not? We share this with you out of love for humanity and to assist you in your ascension process. For it has been foretold for eons that a mass awakening is to occur and a level playing field would be granted to humanity so that humanity could make its own choice about whether it would destroy itself or choose the knowledge it receives to save itself. YOU are all being chosen to discover the truth. The veil has been lifted for all of you. The time of that lifting was prophesied by the Mayan people – also an indigenous tribe who were great time-keepers. Many spoke of the end times, but know this – it was just the beginning of a new age. An age where truth would reign. And 'rain' it has, through the ascension light energies hitting your planet ever since.

The veil we speak of is the one that acts like a curtain between stages. There is no pun here; the stage is real and this really is a story. The ancients call it a dream, but as we have said and will keep on saying, dream time is over; the time of remembering is here. Reconnecting to your heritage, not only through your earthly heritage, through the corridors of time in your past lives, but also from your time in the stars. For there are two shamans, one of the earth, and one of the skies. And it's time for the two to meet so that heaven can meet earth

126

and the golden age can be brought through. There are prophecies of the 144,000 light workers returning to earth to assist humanity. But we want to be clear, they are much more than light workers; they are in fact starseeds, and there is a major difference. Light workers are still working in an old paradigm of duality of good and bad, light and dark, right and wrong. Starseeds know that all is one, just with two sides – like two sides of the one coin. Your Star Wars movies demonstrate this notion well. All along, the truth of your world has been hidden in reverse. The truth is depicted in science fiction and mythology and appears false, but it is so real. And what you have been told is real is the furthest from the truth. Some of you reading this will know this already, and for them, this is like a welcome breath of fresh air. Thank goodness, someone is saying all of this so clearly. Some reading this will have suspected this all long but never breathed a word to anyone else in the fear that they may be seen as crazy.

Some of you have tried to speak out and have been shot down quickly by those still stuck in the paradigm of fear. We urge you to learn about these worlds, the spirit world and the one of soul. Our channel can help and we've asked her to disseminate some of the information she has learnt on her journey in this book.

We like talking about her through her; although she finds it embarrassing, we think it's funny. And we joke at this point to remind you that although these subjects are heavy and enough to make you feel like the rug has been taken out from under you, we want you to know that we are inter-dimensional beings who travel the cosmos freely just like you once did. Some of you have travelled back here to help humanity see the truth, the whole truth and nothing but the truth, to cure you of your insanity. Like Jake Sully in Avatar. You see! You see how the truth is in your films!

Now, we wish to demonstrate an interesting inversion for you. Confused thinking and delusional thoughts are symptom of madness, yes? Well know this and know this well, for as the veil thins more of you, not just the sensitives will see that the REAL beings with confused thinking and delusional thoughts are the dark beings who believe in EVIL. They are the ones who are sick and unwell and deserve compassion and assistance in getting well enough to return home to light also.

Now we have obtained the Key of Truth, it's time to obtain the Key of Perspective.

The Key of Perspective

**Change the way you look at things and
the things you look at change.**

Wayne W. Dyer

Be normal, they say. Don't be too happy or too sad, think too fast or too slow. Just be normal. Be mindful of what you say. Don't speak of bad things or bad events that have happened. It may bring shame; better to keep a secret. Be normal; don't stand out. Don't speak too fast or too slow and don't get too angry. Be normal. Don't bring attention to yourself. Be like everybody else and get a job that pays well, even if you don't like it. Be normal. Having money and security is the most important thing there is. If you are poor, people will look down on you and you are nothing in society. Be normal, don't look too over-the-top, cut your hair like everyone else, and dress well, lest you be labelled as weird. Be normal, go to school and learn like everyone else, even if you think that what you're learning is mindless and not helpful to your future. Even if you think that all your schooling is doing is teaching you to memorise useless facts. Education is important. Just be normal.

Don't tell anyone that you had a funny feeling something would happen. You're not psychic! You don't have a gift, it was just a fluke;

people who know things ahead of time are weird. Be normal, get married and have children. That's what you're supposed to do with your life. The great dream for everyone. Make a family, earn enough to live comfortably, enjoy life and then die. That's what normal people do. Don't strive for anything else. Why would you? Don't take unnecessary risks. Be normal.

Don't tell anyone about the figure you saw out of the corner of your eye. They'll think you're crazy – maybe you are crazy. Don't tell anyone about that dream you had where a divine being spoke to you. Just be normal. Don't pay any attention to that internal voice. Normal people don't hear voices internally or externally. Be normal and don't speak of such things. Get a decent career – something that is going to set you up for life. No-one likes a wanderer. Just be normal. Work hard like everybody else and save lots of money so you can one day retire and then not have to work. Be normal. Don't pay attention to the restlessness. That unhappiness you feel inside is because you're NOT normal. Just be normal.

Phew! That's my rant on how much I dislike the term *normal*. Hopefully my rant illustrates the pressure on all of us to fit a certain standard; to conform to ideas of what is acceptable and all the unspoken rules that govern us. No wonder there is confusion when we step out of order of what's meant to be normal.

The Soul Lens

Our experience is subjective, with no two people seeing the world in the same way. One person could be looking at the world and thinking what a wonderful glorious world we live in, while the next is thinking this world is nuts, crazy and horrible. Same world, different lens. If you imagine putting on a pair of glasses that allowed you to view from the perception of the soul, everything changes. Problems become opportunities, difficulties are challenges, mistakes are for learning, sickness is a blessing and coincidences are divine interventions. You are here on this planet to simply become the best version of you in relationship to yourself and others. That's all there is. There isn't a right relationship, right career, right car, right friends (unless you're hanging around with spiritual riff-raff, of course). My point is we are here to live, learn, love, express, unite and, here's the kicker, *without judgement*. And it's a kicker because humans judge by nature, but the soul doesn't.

If you looked at something, say an object, from a soul view, you would pick it up and inspect it with deep curiosity and absolutely no judgement. Incidentally, this is the same way an ET or alien lifeform would. You would wonder, "What is this? What can I learn from this and what can it be used for?" Looking at your own experiences through the lens of symptomology, without labelling them, can help you see the purpose of your experiences.

As humans, we fear what we don't understand. In this world of conditioning, there is a fear of standing out, of being different, which is further perpetuated by the deeply embedded notion that somehow, being different is wrong. We are all as individual as our fingerprints, like snowflakes, where no two are the same. We think differently, at different speeds, feel differently, at different depths, behave differently according to different values and beliefs. However, we all have the chemical in our brains called oxytocin, which is the belonging chemical that pushes us to seek fulfilment through a sense of likeness. Family, community and fitting in are important to us. To feel misunderstood, judged, ostracised and outcast forms a deep pain in the psyche. Those labelled with a disorder often carry this deep pain like a mark on their soul. Stigma means to be marked. Accepting this label causes even more suffering.

Think of the movie *Happy Feet*. You probably know it, but hear me out on my version of the synopsis. Cute little Mumble (aptly named), is a penguin just like the rest, but appears to be defective due to being dropped before he was born. He can't sing like every other penguin but he's got some weird shit going on with his feet. The community, including his family, ridicule and reject him, including Gloria the chick (well, penguin, actually), who Mumble has a crush on. He finds himself lost, away from his own tribe, and finds solace for a while in another community that embraces him and his weird feet. He then reunites with Gloria and tries to win her affections by pretending to be able to sing (by lip-synching to a back-up singer). Gloria is the kind of penguin that likes to keep it real, so she isn't too impressed. When Mumble finally accepts himself and just does what he does best – tap dance – then he gets accepted and, like all happy endings, becomes a star and gets the girl. Moral of the story: he couldn't sing, but boy, could he dance!

Now, Mumble could have lived up to his name and kept trying to sing, or act like he could, or get depression and anxiety. He could have berated himself and hated the way he was. You seeing my point here? The real key to his success was the help of the outside community who thought his dancing skills were cool! They loved his skills, seeing them as a unique talent. It helped him shift his perspective of being defective to being talented.

In eastern indigenous communities, people exhibiting signs of what the west calls schizophrenia are treated as gifted or chosen ones who are able to bring messages from other worlds. They are taken aside and cared for. Issues they may have are healed in a natural way by connecting to nature. They are trained so that the healer within can emerge. They are guided through an initiation process to become medicine men or women, also known as shamans. They become happy and wise elders.

Super Powers

Our deepest fear is not that we are inadequate. Our deepest fear is that we are powerful beyond measure. It is our light, not our darkness that most frightens us. We ask ourselves, 'Who am I to be brilliant, gorgeous, talented, fabulous? 'Actually, who are you not to be?

Marianne Williamson

What if you could view yourself as different from the norm and that, rather than being less than, this made you special? What if you could turn your so-called deficits into assets? What if you could turn what you see as a curse into a gift? What if you believed that the way you are has its advantages? What if, rather than seeing yourself as disordered, you saw yourself as a super-being with extraordinary talents?

ADD and ADHD, for example, have amazing traits within them that differ from the average person. While most people can focus on one thing quite well, those with these traits are able to take in multiple pieces of information at one time. Like ninjas, they can be aware of their surroundings, listen to a conversation on the other side of the room while doing a task and notice the way the energy has shifted in the room when someone has just walked in. They think fast on their feet, come up with abstract ideas and concepts and see the patterns in everything. This energy, when harnessed, can create a mastermind. With an unwavering acceptance and unique perspective, a person with ADHD traits can turn the perception of a deficit into an unparalleled asset that separates them from their peers as an extraordinary talent.

Perhaps you can see yourself and others with these apparent afflictions as divinely gifted beings, capable of momentous change in a sick society. Embrace yourselves and those around you who 'suffer' with the utmost care and love and believe in yourself or them. Have faith that no matter where you are in your journey, you will find your way if met with non-judgemental curiosity. Viewing the self and others with eyes of unconditional love is key. Unconditional love in this situation means that even though you are weird, different, have strange experiences, and are not making sense to me, I will still love you and endeavour to understand you.

What if you could shift your perspective just a little to see that your differences and ways of being have something to tell you, to show you, to teach you? What if symptoms of a mental health problem are symptoms of a much deeper issue, a symptom of a soul issue? After all, the term 'psychiatry' does mean doctor of the soul!

The Pleiadian Perspective

Depression is a signal, not a disease. Depression is the soul's way of saying, "I'm unhappy with the course and direction of your life". It's time to wake up to the truth. You are not living to your potential and there are some changes to make for you to find fulfilment. This is your reminder or wake-up call to re-evaluate things. If depression could speak, it may say these things. It may say I am not happy with you. This is not what we had planned and I am here to remind you of the plans we made for your life before you were born. Before you were born you made some agreements to fulfil a purpose, but right now you are lost.

You are believing the illusion and lies that you have been fed. Now, of course, we knew you were going to be born into a world of illusion, so you planned for these signals to be sent to you, for you knew that the dissatisfaction that arises within you would be a motivation for you to start your search within you. A search for meaning, a search for truth, a search for you to find value in your life and in yourself. You knew that depression would be your signal to say that you are off your divine soul blueprints course. In your current experience, your depression may trouble you, but from the soul's perspective, when you are troubled you know the only option is to move towards a solution.

However, when there is trouble within you, the solution must be sought from within you. And here lies your lesson. For too long you have sought happiness in things outside of you, your job and your status, in other people, in things that provide temporary enjoyment, and yet you still feel discontent and empty inside. You came here to expand your consciousness and experience and yet you have forgotten. Your depression is a signal and reminder to you that this internal desire cannot be pushed aside anymore.

Your yearning to grow will not disappear because you are in human form, but you are much more than a pleasure-seeking machine. This signal is your desire for fulfilment, to be more, to do more with his life that you have chosen. You are not here by accident. You have chosen to participate in this world in human form to expand your knowledge and to remember the 'being' part of your human being. Perhaps you have become a human doing, sacrificing yourself for others instead of learning the balanced harmony of giving and receiving. Perhaps you have sold your own dreams only to fulfil what others want of you. Perhaps you believe in the things that your caregivers have told you, when it goes against your innermost thoughts and feelings, and you are too afraid to go against the majority. Perhaps you don't want to stand out or feel different. Perhaps when you have shared your dreams for greater things you have been shot down, called crazy, ostracised and you have quit dreaming, quit aspiring because this makes other people uncomfortable.

Perhaps you have adopted this lack of comfortability as your own, yet this discontented stirring within you will not cease. If depression had a voice it would say: I am depression and I am here to remind you of the greatness of who you are and all that you can be!

Anxiety

Anxiety is not a disease, it's a signal. It's a sign to question yourself about whether you are enough, whether what you're dreaming can really be achieved. What will others think? If I am able to do these great things, will I still be loved or will I be judged? Will people think I don't care for them if I achieve success? Will they think of me as being arrogant? There's so much to be afraid of; people are dying and starving in the world. Perhaps I should be content with just getting by? But why is this not enough?

Before you were born, dear ones, you knew that fear was a disease on this planet. You were born crying, were you not? It's a rude shock to be born into a vibration of fear when you were just in a place of pure bliss and unfathomable unconditional love. Yet as a soul you knew you could rise above this, for you have chosen this. However, somewhere along the way you forgot. You forgot your greatness and what you came here to achieve. It is convenient to think of fear as a disorder for you especially. Something is wrong with you, yes, but the problem does not lie within your brain; it lies within your soul. Fear is just as much a personal demon as it is a disease on this planet, but it isn't something that you should own and make your own. It is a vibration operating here but you don't need to be its customer.

Fear is perpetuated in every generation, in almost every belief system, religious and spiritual, and it is broadcast daily to keep you a prisoner. If your eyes were open to the real agenda perpetuated against you, this would be your first lesson. Do not accept it. Do not accept that at the base level, all humans want to do is harm, hurt and kill each other. The human race, when faced with adversity as a whole, would seek to heal and help one another, but you have been trained to believe that this is not the case. Empty your mind of these harmful messages by not allowing yourself to be programmed with violent images and news, and once this is complete you will then have your own personal fears to overcome, and you're halfway there. All that has been passed to you generationally must then be examined. The true nature of what you are must be realised; a powerful sovereign being made of pure consciousness that consists of unconditional love.

You are not too young, old, tall, short, fat, skinny, poor, rich, white, black, yellow or brown for anything. You are who you are without all these labels, and the deconditioning of all these divisions is what your soul truly seeks, to find the unity within and outside of you. To see yourself without these limitations. To release yourself from your own personal judgement perpetuated towards yourself, so then you may be free to aspire, to create and liberate yourself from the illusion of judgement from others. For no-one can truly judge you unless you are judging yourself. No-one can persecute you unless you are first persecuting yourself. Knowledge is seen as the holy grail of progress; however, your soul requires a stripping of the knowledge that has been handed down to you. Perhaps you have been taught to fear blacks, Jews, Muslims, or believe that people are out to hurt you. Perhaps this has been your experience, yet if you could hear your soul, it would tell you that you handpicked these experiences and teachings to debate them within yourself and find your own way. You cannot seek if you are not already lost and you knew you would be entering a realm of duality; you knew you would need to provide yourself with the experience of the polar opposite. It's the same lesson disguised in a different wrapping. Same same but different.

Perhaps you have tried and you have failed; perhaps all you have known is fear or perhaps you are so sensitive that the vibration of fear cripples you. Fear is a part of earth's consciousness and within the fields of duality; it has its place as a great teacher. Fear provides you with an opportunity to face yourself. To face all the misguided beliefs you hold about reality. The unknown of what could and might happen has been taught to you to be out of your control. The truth is that you are creating your reality in each and every moment and knowledge of this creates freedom from fear. Fear is merely the absence of faith. When you claim your divine birthright of being the master of your reality with full faith, fear cannot exist. Life does not happen to you. It is created by you.

And here lies your dilemma. Accept your divine greatness or a palatable response from your medical industry which seeks to keep you ill; that you are disordered in some way and you just need to manage and get by or search deeper within yourself to uncover the real fear. If you could hear your soul, it would say that this fear is your signal to dig. Dig and keep digging until you find its true source. There is great liberty in not accepting that this disease of fear does not truly belong to you but within the systems on your planet designed to enslave you. That you do not need to be a victim of such systems or a victim of your experiences and beliefs that have been perpetuated seemingly against you. Your fear is telling you to get up, rise up and be all that you can be. Fear is not the enemy or a disorder; make fear your friend and allow it to work with you and for you. Same same but different.

Psychosis

Psychosis isn't a malady; it's the body's natural coping tool to an outer reality that doesn't make sense to the soul. It is also a calling. A calling to live between and in two worlds, the real and non-real. If your soul could speak to you about psychosis, it would say your trilogy of movies, titled The Matrix, is a very real depiction of what you are in and the soul knows this. It is ironic, therefore, that most labelled with this disorder are asked to swallow a 'pill'. These pills from your medical industry are designed to silence the outrageous notions of such non-real, non-physical worlds, and drive the 'affected' into submission to accept the only reality being provided to them. A chemical thought restraint.

However, there isn't only one world as you have been taught to believe; there are worlds within worlds within worlds. Schizophrenia is often an outer experience of the deep psychic soul pain of being forced to live within lies and distortions. The schizophrenic is really what you could call a multi-dimensional experiencer, whose senses are tuned into the non-physical realms both inter-dimensionally and intra-psychically. Your mainstream systems say that these experiences are not real, which further perpetuates the soul pain and drives the soul traveller deeper into despair. The most ancient and oldest souls of all know the truth, feel the truth, embody the truth of all worlds combined and have chosen pre-birth, the most difficult soul path of all! To help the integration of all worlds into unity, to assist the bringing in and merging of higher realms, which you may call heaven, into lower realms through their own personal 'experience' – experience being a science experiment, if you will, of what it is to experience the full knowing of ALL TRUTH in one's divine soul blueprint.

The term multi-dimensional experience (MDE) could be described as a trip or a journey into unknown lands; the lands which this world sees as fantasy, where the fabric of consciousness comes alive and thought forms coexist across all planes. Where animals and plants can communicate, where travel is not defined by country but by time, where such things as telepathy, teleportation and other life forms reside, where the self exists in the past, present and future simultaneously and those voices are parts of the self, co-existing in those multiple places. While these experiences hold great truth in the realms of possibility, they clash with the mainstream beliefs that such things cannot exist, and where inner conflict occurs, there is outer affliction.

To carry such truth within, whilst living in an external world filled with untruths, lies and distortions, is what perpetuates the real malady. This label given to you by your health 'care' professionals is a direct mirror image of an illusion that blames the soul traveller as deluded. The delusions they are apparently suffering are illusions created by this system. Look around you at what has happened to all indigenous communities historically. They have been maimed, killed, with an attempt at total eradication of the people, the systems, beliefs and ideologies. What do ALL indigenous people believe in? Non-physical realities and dimensions. These communities lived at one time in perfect harmony with one another and with the earth. They all lived freely as sovereign beings, not enslaved by systems. There has been a great divide between ancient wisdom, knowledge and truth and the nature of the soul has been forgotten in modern society.

Multi-dimensional experiencers have the ability to travel through time and space through their consciousness, a skill well known in shamanic indigenous communities. Ironically, your science fields have quantified this notion through quantum physics, openly discussing the reality that we live in a multi-dimensional world. Yet, when someone lives this out, it is not seen as a phenomena to be understood and integrated, but one to be shackled and restrained. Past lives, ghosts, demons, curses, light beings, master teachers and creator architects do not belong in a world of logic but one of fantasy and delusion in the medical world.

Modern psychiatry has not changed much at all since its inception. In the beginning, the disordered were physically beaten and shackled, and now they are chemically shackled and numbed into submission. Same same but different.

Armed with the Key of Perspective, it's time to obtain the Key of Alignment.

The Key of Alignment

Drop the idea of becoming someone, because you are already a masterpiece. You cannot be improved. You have only to come to it, to know it, to realise it.

Osho

I Am That I Am

Ten years ago, I was researching consciousness and manifestation in an attempt to understand my own experiences because I was seeing synchronicities everywhere. I had a suspicion that my psychic messages and channelling abilities were coming completely from the right part of my brain, the creative, imaginative side. Someone had recommended I watch a TED talk by Jill Bolte Taylor. Jill was a neuroscientist who had a stroke, and has since fully recovered and written a book called *My Stroke of Insight*. She has done extensive studies on the human brain and its relation to mental health. The insight she refers to in her TED talk was realising that when she lost all her faculties to move and speak, she also became aware as an observer of her own experience that she was also feeling a total state of bliss and enlightenment when she appeared to be completely in her right brain hemisphere.

As I watched this, I suddenly lost my ability to speak. Yes, you read that right. I actually began to experience what she was talking about while I was watching the footage! Similar to her experience, I also felt the bliss and complete contentment of the euphoric feeling of having no attachment to anything through my left brain. My partner at the time had come to sit next to me on the lounge and so I wrote to him on paper what I was experiencing and tried to get him to watch some of the TED talk.

If he had not been there to witness my experience, I may have labelled my experience as somewhat crazy. Being the jokester and comedian that I am, he immediately thought I was joking and asked me to just stop it and start talking. I remember writing down that this was serious, but to stay calm because this was all happening for a higher reason. I told him on paper that this experience would be included in this book!

As he was talking to me I had a childlike fascination with his lips moving and how he was forming words. I felt like a newborn baby who was watching adults around them speaking and I was in a state of complete joy and delight. I was constantly laughing and giggling and totally enjoying myself. No wonder babies look like they're having the time of their lives. Because of Jill's talk, I knew exactly where I was, completely in the right side of my brain. I had no care in the world and was completely in each moment as it arose. Just like Jill, I also was aware of the experience as well as the observer.

After a while my partner became a little irritated, asking me to come back, but I didn't want to come back. I wrote to him, "Come on, babe, why don't you come here with me? All you have to do is be in your right mind. Get it? Be in your right mind?" I laughed hysterically at my own pun. He wasn't too impressed and I knew I would have to come back. I had no idea how that was going to happen, but without an ounce of fear I intuitively knew I had to learn how to speak through him. I wrote to him asking him to just keep talking with me about anything. I concentrated fully on the formation that his lips would make when he spoke. It took a lot of effort and mental concentration, but with all the energy and focus I could muster I blurted out one word, which was "I".

I was super excited about it just like a child would be. I was clapping and smiling and felt so proud of myself. I wrote that I wanted him to sing something. I watched the shape of his lips forming words intently once more and the next word I was able to get out was "do". Once again, just like a baby I was so pleased I could say do, and to challenge myself I tried stringing them together and found myself happily pacing the lounge room reciting, "I do, I do, I do".

My partner, being as much of a jokester as I was, smiled at me and said, "Okay great, will you marry me then?" We both had a laugh and then I noticed something interesting. I realised that when I said "I do", I was actually doing what I wanted to do, which was to speak.

Then, like a lightning bolt, I was guided by some knowing within me, without a shadow of a doubt, that if I could just say the words *I am* three times, I would be completely back in both parts of my brain and able to speak. I then wrote to him asking him to keep reciting the word am or use sentences with that word in it, and after a few minutes of dedicated concentration, I spoke the words, "I am, I am, I am" and I was instantly back.

I would like to say I was relieved; I think my partner was more relieved than I was because I suddenly had a significant migraine that felt like it was cutting through the centre of my brain. I had to have three days off work after that, unable to see properly or tolerate any bright lights. At the time I did not realise the gravity of the experience and its relation to creation and the *I am* presence. The power of the *I am* statement was being shown to me in the way that I was able to bring myself back into full consciousness, into both parts of my brain, just by saying *I am*.

The *I am* consciousness comes from the story in history of the response given by God to Moses when God instructed him to go and free the Israelites from Egypt. Moses asks, "Who am I to go and just do such a thing and whom shall I say sent me?" and so Moses asks God his name. His response was, 'ehyeh 'ăšer 'ehyeh, which translates to "I am that I am". How many times have you heard in spiritual circles that one must find out who they are? Who you are is God in human form. Who you are is not attached to anything but God. When we are aligned to this universal truth, that you are a part of everything, and therefore are everything, then you can find peace. You are not God the almighty creator of everything, but born from and part of God as a whole, so whenever you hear yourself saying, "But who am I to do this?" then remember you are a God, just same same but different.

Harmony isn't when you have all your ducks in a row. What kind of saying is that anyway? Where does that come from? It is a saying about alignment, yes, meaning that when everything is falling into place or everything is going your way, then you'll be happy. This saying perpetuates a belief that once the alignment outside of you is complete and in a row, then you can have harmony. Yet it is the alignment within you that is required. The heart that is closed is out of alignment. Are you starting to see how each door that has been unlocked with these keys affects one another? Without harmony, there cannot be alignment.

How many of you, when feeling depressed and in a rut, complain that you don't have motivation? Then you wait. You wait and wish you just had the motivation. As strange as this sounds, motivation is waiting for you to be motivated so that it can come and 'be' with you! This is what alignment is all about. God speaks of this through Neale Donald Walsch in his book *Conversations with God*. It is the concept of being, doing and having; you must first be in the vibration of what you want, do the things that bring this in, and then the having is the combination of the being and doing. It really is that simple. You just choose to be motivated and the rest follows. It's hard to comprehend something so simple because we have been conditioned to struggle.

Another popular thing in the spiritual wave has been to use affirmations – for example, I am lovable, I am prosperous. Most of us know that our thoughts are creating our reality. Whenever we are lacking faith in ourselves or being critical, we are affirming the very path our lives will take. That's how powerful we are. The power of the statement 'I am' is not always understood. *To say 'I am' in a declaration is the power of alchemy of bringing spirit to matter.* I never really understood this completely until I was able to integrate a very strange experience I had.

The Universe is Always Listening

I was regretting the past and fearing the future. Suddenly my Lord was speaking: "My name is I Am". He paused. I waited. He continued. "When you live in the past, with its mistakes and regrets, it is hard. I am not there. My name is not I WAS. When you live in the future, with its problems and fears, it is hard. I am not there. My name is not I WILL BE. When you live in this moment it is not hard. I am here. My name is I AM."

Helen Mallicoat

The soul, just like the body, is a self-regulating system. It will seek to align itself, even with you trying to get in the way. Think of driving a vehicle and someone else taking the wheel. This is who you are at times. The crazy person who wants to take the wheel and cause an accident when really the direction you were going in was fine all along. You might be experiencing problems at work which cause you a great deal of stress and wonder what is happening. But you forgot that you have been wishing and hoping to find something better. In fact, you've been thinking that you may start your own business. In desperation one morning, you said under your breath, "God, help me get out of this damn job!" But somehow you don't make the connection that the problems at work have been created by the god within you, for you, to develop the courage you need to quit and take a risk.

There is a saying, "Be careful what you wish for, because you just might get it". Some people experience this almost instantly, and for them this is great. For others it feels like the Universe or God is playing a cruel joke and they lose all faith, when in reality they are still receiving what they asked for, it's just taking a bit longer because they are not in alignment! Here are some examples.

You may have asked for a loving relationship, but if you are not ready for one, to be part of the love that you desire, what will come to you is an experience that may prepare you, a relationship that may teach you forgiveness and consist of betrayal, because you may not see yourself as worthy or lovable.

You may ask for a wake-up call, and you may be provided with an unusual set of circumstances that causes you to question your reality and be confronted with ego-deflating experiences that hurt like hell, but in the long run they are helping you to really wake up to the truth of you so you can begin manifesting your life from a heart space. You may ask for more friendships but then become disheartened in the ones you have because you may need to learn that like attracts like, and you must first become that which you want to attract and be a better friend to others. You may ask for relief from stress only to fall ill, so that you may learn that the key to better health is to stop and rest from time to time.

When you are asking for 'things', then the universe will send you the experience you need to gain the 'qualities' you will need to obtain those things. It's best to ask for qualities such as courage, patience, tolerance, commitment, faith and forgiveness, for example, all the while staying open to the lessons being presented to you which will come through your life experiences. We go to so many professionals for assistance when we are looking to help ourselves. There is nothing wrong with that, as long as they seek to empower you and not foster dependence. Because you are your greatest asset and no-one knows you better than you! Fostering a relationship with yourself is the biggest gift you can give to yourself, and it is therefore wise to include this in your list of self-care activities, such as eating well, etc.

Metatron has asked to share his wisdom on alignment for this chapter. At first, I argued – no, just kidding. I said, "Sure, be my guest".

Metatron

The key to alignment is not about ducks. Yes, I can confirm that. How is that for some wisdom? Now we know what it isn't, let's look at what it is. Alignment means to be in line with where it is you want to go, or how you want to be or feel. And yes, just like a car, if its wheels are out of alignment, it's going to be hard to steer and stay on course to get to its destination. This is how many of you are. Struggling with the wheel of life, with all your 'symptoms', when all that is needed is a simple alignment. So, let's get aligned!

Wouldn't it be great if we could just bring you all in for an alignment? Imagine that! Beaming you up like in Star Trek to sort you out and drop you back so you could continue your life with all your ducks in a row. If I sound sarcastic, then your intuition is spot on. Indeed I joke because from where I am amongst many others, we often wish we could beam you up and make the necessary alterations. The age-old question of why God allows bad things to happen comes into play here, so let's get one thing straight. Allowing is done by you, not by God. You decided to have this experience as a soul at some point or another. Some of you have been trapped for a very long time so deep into soul amnesia and the density of the earth plane that you cannot even begin to recognise the magnificent powerful creator you are. This soul amnesia is lifting for many of you, and there are many now activating yourselves for this time to awaken and really take the blinkers off.

And then there are those who remember and are helping others to remember too. Whichever category you fall into, make no mistake that you are right where you need to be at this time. There is a natural order being returned to this earth by ways of divine intervention, you could say, to ensure that the free will you have that has caused so much destruction in the first place can be skewed back on course to ensure a planetary alignment to keep your planet on course!

I am Metatron, and although it has been written about me that I was once a scribe named Enoch, then an archangel called Metatron, I also work closely as an interface between the angelic realms and the galactic realms. For planetary alignment, getting you in line away from self-destruction means we need to help you closer to the earth's field from the angelic realm for you to find personal alignment. Make no mistake that there are many of you who have been on your personal development journeys for a long time, and that's a great thing and I can't exactly beam you up for an alignment because of the laws of free will, but I can speak to you through divine intervention through this channel who is writing, and be so bold as to ask you a question.

Has your self-development journey been about you or what you want to have? Think about that for a moment. Just stop and ponder. If it's been about what you want to have, then bang, right there, you're out of alignment. But what's wrong with wanting to have love, wanting to have abundance, wanting to have closer relationships, wanting to have fame, even? Here's a truth that will assist you. If you're trying to drive to the 'have' island, you'll never get there. It simply doesn't exist. It's one of those spiritual illusions people keep talking about, like fear.

Now what if I told you that the key to having is being? To have love you must first be it; to have abundance you must first be it. Those of you who have researched the art of manifestation may be starting to recognise this. Why of course, many of the great spiritual teachers have spoken about this. Now do you want to drive to the 'being' island? What if I said you would never get there, either? Think about it – it's an island! You can't drive there; you'd have to get a boat! Ha ha, but of course!

So, we've gone from comparing you to a car that needs a wheel alignment to a boat that needs to get to the island of 'being'. The difference is that to get to its destination, the boat doesn't really get 'driven'; it simply gets steered there! And how many of you are so driven, so determined, so ambitious about achieving your goals? If only I do this, if I get this, have this plan, do this course, get this job, then surely I'll have what I want. This is the conditioning that has run you into the very ground. Let go of all this conditioning and be open to a new way of being.

How do I be something I don't have yet? Isn't that fake? How am I supposed to be happy when I'm depressed? How am I supposed to feel like being social when I'm anxious and want to be alone? How do I be joyful when I feel the opposite? Stop believing you have to have something in order to be something and then you will be able to have it. Waiting for happiness to be able to do things is futile. Allow yourself to just be happy. Choose it. This may sound so simplistic, especially to those of you who experience great pain at the hands of depression and even to the channel I write through. What if you are in a world of pain – can you just choose not to be? The answer is yes. The biggest illusion of all time is that you have no choice. It's deeply embedded in you, not only from deep conditioning here on this planet but from other lifetimes where you may have resided in star systems where there was no free will. There were no choices to be made because beings just did what they did out of an automatic alignment. They didn't have a mind of their own; they were all plugged into one collective mind at all times. That collective mind held the resonance of all truth.

You are all connected to a universal mind also, all plugged in; however, your collective mind that you have been plugged into is not connected to all truth. The matrix you are plugged into has been polluted and distorted and we, meaning me and the rest of us on the 'higher' realms, are assisting in all the ways we can to bring the truth back into the collective mind of earth. We would love for you to meet us halfway by realising and really owning that each day you are choosing your state, you choose your way of being in the world. No-one else has created it, no-one else has caused it, and what you want to have is within your being already, so just be it. You are your own master. Don't be a puppet to the matrix of distortion out there.

Here's a daily mantra that you can decide to use if you wish. It's your choice!

Today I choose to be in the vibration of joy, peace, happiness and harmony. I choose loving thoughts about myself and others because I know that choosing this brings me towards everything that I love. I choose to be the love that I wish to see in the world because I know I form part of the world and therefore I am the world, and I mean the world to everyone out there. Today I choose acceptance that when I notice I am out of alignment of the truth I really am, that I can allow those feelings to arise and have their place but I need not dwell in them. That when I allow them space to breathe, they will then dissipate as fast as they arose within me. Feelings come and go like waves on the ocean, and I am merely the boat staying aligned on the surface. I can steer myself to safety or be smashed by the rough seas. It's my choice because I'm the captain of my ship and I choose the island of being, which means I can be where I want to be at all times. Today I choose to be in the vibration of joy, peace, happiness and harmony and I know that if tomorrow is like today, I'll always be where I want to be. All I have is today and so I choose joy, peace, happiness and harmony.

Armed with the Key of Alignment, it's time to obtain the Key of Forgiveness.

The Key of Forgiveness

Forgiveness is one of the most powerful frequencies on the planet. If you're looking for freedom, this is where it's at.

If you have the key of alignment and really want to create things in your life and have the personal freedom to do so, you need the key of forgiveness. The ascension process requires us to not only raise our vibration, but our frequency. Our frequency is like our sound signature that reverberates through the cosmos. If it is polluted with anger, pain or resentment, it basically sounds like an annoying car horn. If it is harmonious, it sounds like a heavenly chorus of angels. Creation started with sound. The cosmos is a symphony orchestra, with each of us playing our own instrument. Your instrument is you!

From what I have seen, forgiveness has to be the biggest healing process known to mankind. Forgiveness affords us grace and grace is the highest blessing there is. In all the years I have been involved in healing work, not only for myself but with others, what I have witnessed through the process of forgiveness has never been short of miraculous. It has the power to transmute the lowest of energies and create real shifts in thoughts and behaviours, not only for the person releasing, but for the people being forgiven. It truly liberates both parties and frees them to zero point or neutral energy, which can be best described as the point of no friction. When there is no friction energetically, the situation is healed. I have also seen the power of forgiveness in the spirit world where earthbound spirits who are stuck are suddenly free and drawn to the light.

Forgiveness is essential when you are awakening and ascending because these processes shift your worldview, but the unrefined ego, through its duality consciousness, reeks of judgement and blame. When you suddenly see the real state of the world and the way others are living, you may find yourself angry at all the horrible meat-eating humans if you're a vegan, or you may be angry at the government for taking away your sovereign rights, or you may be angry at the discovery that the money system is designed to enslave you; you may be angry ... well, you get the point! There is a lot to be angry about, but if you stay angry and don't accept that everything else will have its own natural unfoldment in its own divine timing, then all you are really doing is adding to the shit you are judging in the first place by being that really annoying car horn in the traffic!

Radical Responsibility

Life is simple. Everything happens for you, not to you. Everything happens at exactly the right moment, neither too soon nor too late. You don't have to like it ... it's just easier if you do.

Byron Katie

Radical responsibility is aptly named because it supports the radical notion that you are indeed responsible not only for your feelings, but for everything that happens to you. It's not about self-blame, but the ability to respond to what you are creating and hence the cause. Being responsible for what is happening in your personal world and all of your experiences means you are creating all of it! It's a hard pill to swallow (no pun intended – well, maybe it was) but here's an example.

If your boss is being really harsh to you and is always critical of you, then you are creating this. How? There is a part of you that believes you are not worthy of positive encouragement and being recognised for your work, and they are mirroring back to you how critical you are of yourself. Because this is the shadow aspect of yourself and it's hard for you to see it, you then blame the other and it's suddenly their fault you are experiencing it. It's not their fault but they are the trigger, and before it's too late you shoot the messenger without receiving the message. What is unhealed in you is the self-criticism. Heal the way you criticise yourself and the belief that you need to be criticised, and the outer experience will leave you.

Living in this way isn't easy, even when you know this principle. When I had a string of bullying incidents in my workplace, my therapist at the time asked me to have a think about what it was within me that was creating these experiences. I remember thinking, "Are you nuts? Why would I be creating this; how is this my fault?" It wasn't till much later that I could see the patterns within me creating the outer reality. Blame is so deeply embedded in the fabric of our society that radical responsibility appears as madness to most. It sits in our group consciousness as normal and therefore socially acceptable. Recognise these? "You made me feel angry", or "Of course I'm upset, what did you expect?" or "No-one ever appreciates me". These are the hallmarks of disempowered thinking which create personal suffering and only serve to keep you stuck, recreating the same issue with different people. Radical responsibility holds three basic premises:

◊ No-one's behaviour is ever about you.

◊ You cannot make anyone feel anything.

◊ No-one can make you feel anything.

If you have never checked out the work of Byron Katie and you identify as someone with victimhood tendencies from your childhood, it may be worth looking at her teachings which support radical responsibility to help you find truth and accountability in your own life. Blaming another person means you're giving your power away. This leads to tiredness, grumpiness and, when left unchecked with other life stresses – voila! You're chronically depressed and wondering if a pill can fix some chemical imbalance.

Resentment

If you apply radical responsibility to resentments, you will find that resentments are just you being angry with yourself, not the other. Resentment is just re-feeling anger over and over again, and you are just re-sending anger towards someone else when it's meant for you. Re-sent-meant!

Chronic fatigue, depression and anxiety are often results of carrying around layers of anger, blame and resentment. Carrying so much of this stuff actually makes you topple over like a heavily laden truck. You simply fall and can't function properly. A good question to ask is, "How am I creating this situation?" I can't stress enough how important it is to make sure you don't use any blame in this whatsoever. Blame has no place in anything, only responsibility does. Self-forgiveness is equally as important as self-blame and anger turned inwards, which is another main contributor to depression.

Ho'oponopono: I Love You, I'm Sorry, Please Forgive Me, Thank You

The following story is true, as evidenced by Dr Joe Vitale. It's the story about a therapist in Hawaii, Dr Ihaleakala Hew Len, who cured a complete ward of criminally insane patients without ever seeing any of them. The psychologist would study an inmate's chart and recite the words, "I love you, I'm sorry, please forgive me, thank you".

The therapist was using a Hawaiian healing process called ho'oponopono. It's based on the premise that anything you want to heal outside of your life starts with healing what's within you.

The Hawaii State Hospital where Dr Hew Len worked was a dangerous place to work and psychologists quit on a monthly basis. The most interesting part was that he never actually saw the patients; he simply reviewed their files and as he looked at those files, he would work on himself. As he worked on himself, patients began to heal.

Patients that had to be shackled were allowed to walk freely, while others who had to be heavily medicated were getting off their medications, and the lost causes who never had a chance of ever being released were being freed. In addition, absenteeism and turnover disappeared.

Dr Len's message may be quite hard to believe, yet it's amazingly simple. He states that we are all responsible for everything that we see in our world. By taking full personal responsibility and then healing the wounded places within ourselves, we can literally heal ourselves and our world. Whenever a place for healing presents itself in your life, both for yourself and for others, open to the place where the hurt resides within you. After identifying this place, with as much feeling as you can, say the following four statements:

◊   I love you.

◊   I'm sorry.

◊   Please forgive me.

◊   Thank you.

The Pleiadians on Forgiveness

Forgiveness is essential to wellbeing, because of the inter-connectivity between you and the other. It is has been said by the channel in this book that the universe is a mirror, a reflection, and this is true; however, there is an inter-connectedness also between each and every human on the planet. We could describe it as an energy field or line that connects all of you. When you are expressing hate and anger towards someone else, you are filling that energy field with toxicity, but that toxicity flows back to you because of the connection.

Some of you know these as cords, and a well-known practice in spiritual circles has been to cut these cords so that the energy flow cannot continue between you and the other person.

This is an inefficient attempt at disconnecting yourself from an illusionary source of pain. That person is not causing you pain; you are. To disconnect the cord is not solving the issue in any way but only robbing yourself of a lesson. Cutting cords is a forceful way to create a neutralised energy. A neutralised energy heals the process but the real neutralisation is forgiveness. The state of unforgiveness works exactly like a set of shackles. It restricts you and the other person from moving on. There is no peace for both parties. But what of the person with no remorse? Surely it is better to just cut cords with such a toxic person if they do not even seek forgiveness. Well, this isn't the best idea either.

Remember we said earlier that you are all connected in energy as an entire race of people on this planet. Well, your state of unforgiveness affects the whole. You withhold your forgiveness because the person isn't sorry, then they go on in an injured state, moving on to hurt others. There's a saying that states, "Hurt people hurt people". Wouldn't it make more sense that fewer hurt people out there walking around meant fewer hurting people on the planet? If you are not hurt inside, you have more love to give, and don't we need to heal this planet? We mean, you might be reading this book to essentially heal yourself, but what for? Do you think your happiness is just about finding happiness? Or is it about sharing it with others, causing happiness to multiply?

When you forgive, you create freedom for yourself and the other. This is true in both the physical and non-physical worlds. The state of unforgiveness creates stagnation, and forgiveness allows a sense of flow; a sense of harmony. So, forgive all and do so with an open heart, even those who do not know the harm they cause. The forgiveness energy still permeates their being although they are not conscious of it, and you are creating harmony for yourself and the pool of consciousness of which you are a part.

Lastly, self-forgiveness is the biggest key to your liberation from internal pain and anguish. The illusion of being wrong and requiring punishment is one of the biggest diseases on this planet. Being wrong, finding blame and assigning a punishment – none of these are helpful in changing anything or learning anything new. It only seeks to keep you locked in a cycle of rinse and repeat and has contributed to your karmic cycle going round and round. It is deeply embedded in your psyche from the justice system created in your world to maintain control.

Do you remember your popular 1970s TV show Get Smart? *Maxwell Smart is a spy who works for 'control' while their enemy spy agency is called 'chaos'. A great comedy show, especially with the irony that Maxwell Smart isn't very smart at all, and is often causing chaos with his lack of insight and control! We mention this because it is important for you to know that, just like in the show, where there is control, chaos is not far behind!*

Control is a dense, dark, lower vibrational energy that is destructive. It does nothing to bring resolution or harmony or change to a situation. Control is in direct violation of the spiritual law of free will, that everyone has a choice to choose how to behave. You do have the power to influence, however, and make something seem more or less pleasing, but leaving the choice open is the best way forward for harmony to prevail.

With self-responsibility and empowerment, your rise to greatness will also see that you will uncover the ways in which you have harmed yourself in the past. You may realise you have been someone who has inadvertently caused great harm to others, realising your feelings of dissatisfaction with the other were really about you not facing you. The sensitive empaths will feel this as a great heavy burden of pain within their hearts. Remember that self-forgiveness is the key to your liberation of moving forward. You live in a world where you have been led to believe that mistakes require punishment. Living by this unconscious belief will only see you trapped in the cycle of personal misery.

Mistakes require rectification. Learning from mistakes, however, can only be done through the heart, not the head. It is important to feel the error of your ways but not dwell in guilt and remorse. Instead, exchange these emotions for determination and hope that you can live in better ways. Always be gentle with yourself, always. Being gentle with you is an art form cultivated by self-forgiveness. Know that the ways in which you have lived do not need to be repeated; there is always a new path ahead because you are the one creating it. Create it with a sense of peace that you are well on your way home.

Now we have unlocked the
Key of Forgiveness, it's time
for the Key of Harmony.

The Key of Harmony

Where there is righteousness in the heart, there is beauty
in the character. When there is beauty in the character,
there is harmony in the home. When there is harmony
in the home, there is order in the nation. When there
is order in the nation, there is peace in the world.

APJ Abdul Kalam

The Goddess Kali

During my time in India, I had only briefly read about the goddess
known as Kali. She was known to me only as the great destroyer and
the goddess of death. Until I felt her presence, I wasn't really aware of
how her energies worked. Boy, was I in for a surprise. After visiting
one of the dedicated Kali temples to meditate early one morning, I
felt her presence walking beside me down the quiet village street.
Instantly I was filled with awe and a fearful reverence I had never
experienced. My heart began beating faster, and I almost became
unable to breathe. To put it bluntly, I was shitting myself. I silently
communicated to her that I was glad she was there and asked her
to teach me, and then she was gone. Besides seeing her present at a
Puja ritual I did with the town priest in the village, I didn't feel her
presence again until I was on the plane back home to Australia.

This time, she felt more like a loving and nurturing mother figure and she told me that she had chosen to work with me and help me reclaim my divine feminine qualities I had so graciously been asking for during my meditations. She went on to give me some motherly advice, which led to streams of tears rolling down my face on the plane because of the fact that I had never really experienced what it was like to be nurtured, loved and guided in this way from my own mother, and I had recently been separated from her under unforeseeable circumstances and I was feeling a great painful hole in my heart.

Researching later, I discovered that Kali brings the death of the ego as the illusory self-centred view of reality. Before I had left for India, I knew that I was seeing more and more ego in those around me and because I am a reflection of the universe, I knew my own ego was being reflected back to me. I had been asking the universe to liberate me from the limitations of my ego and learn how to reclaim my divine femininity, and it appeared the universe had answered me. I also laughed when I learnt that a person who is attached to his or her ego will not be receptive to Mother Kali and she will appear in a fearsome form. It explained why I shat myself the first time I encountered her. I then found out that a mature soul who engages in spiritual practice to remove the illusion of the ego sees Mother Kali as very sweet, affectionate, and overflowing with incomprehensible love for her children, and this confirmed for me that the spiritual rituals I had engaged in had come to fruition.

She has stayed with me ever since, guiding me further and bringing light to the fact when I am operating in ego. I know this because of her shift in energy. She is quite reprimanding when I have behaved foolishly, and when I become humble she has lovingly guided me towards a new way of being. She is teaching me about the divine feminine and seeing myself as a goddess; guiding me into a higher and more spiritual divine form of the feminine, showing me the Holy Grail energies within my body. Although I am way past what you would describe as a girl, I feel like I left Australia a girl and returned a woman, with much more self-love and empowerment.

In this way, Kali is a great teacher and I am her faithful student, and I have seen quite quickly what happens when I haven't taken her advice. Powerful and humbling lessons take place, as I always remember to remain the student and teacher simultaneously. It is interesting to note that it was she who explained a paranormal experience to me on my last night in India. I had awoken all of a sudden in a fright, and felt three ET beings pulling their hands out from behind my eyes and I felt like they had flipped a switch behind my eyes. I had seen Bhagavan Nityananda standing in the doorway, but Kali was nowhere to be seen. Despite my many paranormal experiences, I still have a somewhat academic and analytical mind and the need to understand things and how it all works, and this one baffled me.

So I consulted with Kali. She explained to me that a switch had been inserted within me to see through the lens of fifth-dimensional consciousness, to be able to see myself clearly with higher vibrational unconditional love energies and it was an energetic upgrade. Funnily enough, in the spirit of synchronicity, I later stumbled upon another channeler, 'Pixie Magenta', on YouTube who talked about a code download that starseeds would have recently received and which she described as a 'switch'! The channel stated: "After moving through the Equinox Golden Gateway, many starseeds have begun to activate a certain codex within the DNA structure which is a powerful key code ... We call this *The Kali Activation*". You have to love confirmation like that. Goose-bump material right there!

When it comes to harmony, interpersonal relationships are probably the most difficult things to master and a great cause of emotional pain on the planet. Wounded souls are walking around everywhere with stored grief and hurt, which gets projected out to the world and to those closest to us. You may find yourself falling into the illusion of seeking outside of yourself what you want to fulfil within through your relationship with others. As we shift from the old paradigm of power and control, we are entering a new paradigm of the divine flow of unconditional love rising. The relational psychiatric disorders such as borderline personality disorder and narcissistic personality disorder are labels, the symptoms of which run through all of us across the spectrum. These labels are placed on people; however, the real disorder lies in the social conditioning of men and women everywhere.

The Divine Feminine and Masculine

I think we need the feminine qualities of leadership, which include attention to aesthetics and the environment, nurturing, affection, intuition and the qualities that make people feel safe and cared for.

Deepak Chopra

Harmony can be viewed as balance of all things interconnected by the natural flow of giving and receiving. In spiritual contexts, giving is seen as the masculine energies and receiving is the feminine. As part of the earth's ascension, the divine feminine energies are increasing. The earth herself, being feminine in nature, is having her own kundalini awakening. We are in a great time for feminine energies to lead the way for the doorways of the heart space to open so that harmony can prevail.

However, this isn't about the battle of the sexes! This is about balancing the divine feminine within us all, as we all contain this aspect within us despite our physical sex. This is the time to return to our hearts so we can have internal peace. For as it is above, so it is below; as it is within, so it is without. The outer always reflects the inner, and leading from our masculine sides has taken us through the industrial and technological age, but for peace and harmony to reign, it's time for the heart to lead. Men are just as intuitive as women, but the social conditioning of men to be seen as weak if they show their feelings stops them from expressing it. This quality isn't limited to men, because women who have had histories of abuse and trauma have also learnt ways in which to shut down their emotions and not express them.

With vulnerability perceived as weak and intuition seen as crazy, these energies are calling us to rise above this conditioning as these two things perceived as feminine in nature are the very things that will help us return to love. It's time for women to lead the way for men to their hearts by being more in their divine feminine. The leading is a masculine energy, but for men to truly find their divine masculine, the women must lead the way first because they are the only ones who can, as they hold the resonance of the heart energy more in their physical bodies. Out of a reactionary response from decades of female oppression, the ways in which women have de-masculinised men have been operating for too long, with men running from the very thing they also seek. Yes, there has been a great oppression of women, but men's hearts are also bleeding for this connection. The whole planet is bleeding for the heart connection! The rising from oppression into liberation starts from unconditional love and being in a state of allowing the masculine energies in all of us to drop into the heart space.

Non-Duality

The global shift into higher consciousness is pulling all of us into a personal journey of unification within. Collectively, the mass unification process allow us to merge the heavenly states into the earth grid. This journey that is occurring means we cannot take our baggage with us. All limiting beliefs, judgements and fears held internally are being disrupted and brought to the surface to be released. Arguing from a place of duality and separation will become increasingly uncomfortable, with more ego-loss experiences occurring.

In the third dimension, the feminine and masculine has been split into two separate energies when really, they are one. The very seeds of creation call for these energies to be united for anything to manifest. How many times have you had the creative idea or insight but lacked the determination and drive to put it into action? Or have you put things into action with no idea or insight about where it's going? True inner harmony is to receive and give graciously to ourselves.

The ascension shift we are experiencing means that the masculine, the world of order, control, analysing, organising, planning and calculating will humbly take a back seat. Again, this is not about who is best, or first or last, and from the cosmic perspective, this is the biggest joke of all, for there is NO first or last, no beginning or end, no chicken or egg. Essentially, one equals two! If we replaced every 'or' with 'and' we would be able to heal the split that has operated in our consciousness. The chicken AND the egg are one and the same, just in different form. Same same but different.

The only thing that is different is TIME. The unified field is here and there is no need to take turns to be one or the other, but both simultaneously. As we are collapsing into the time of NOW, you will start to see that you are both male and female and these two energies are not separate, and for harmony to reign they need to be perceived and operated as such.

When this split is healed, a new revelation will prevail – that heaven is here. It's not a place; it's a state of being, of vibration, of frequency, and travel to and from this place is not limited to the illusion of the death portal. It will be revealed that you can easily access and know this state in the non-physical. And as you access it through your hearts, your minds will follow and you will draw down to you and bring that state here and now to your physical reality. And this can only be anchored in the ways you learn to love yourself, and this way of being collectively brings in what is referred to by the ancients as the golden age.

Money and Love

Financial success and abundance are often chased, but it is in the feminine energy of receiving that creates abundance. If your heart is closed to receiving, then you are closed off from abundance. Both money and love are forms of exchange. What blocks you from receiving? Receiving puts you in a state of humility. When others from your past have abused your trust or you have had traumatic experiences, your walls have gone up, which prevent you from receiving anything as your reactions of self-preservation keep you in self-sufficiency mode. You become more comfortable in the masculine left-brained way of giving to afford yourself a feeling of control. To receive graciously, you need to heal the parts within you that are keeping these walls up.

The old adage has been to think before you speak or do, but it's time to feel first, before you speak and do. The masculine has ruled the head and the arena of thought, all the while trying to suppress and control the feelings. All of the right-brained frequencies are coming online. Feeling, sensing, creating, imagining, wondering, observing and allowing. The new cycle brings in the breaking down of this division; the competition between the sexes that has been in battle throughout the ages has divided the very core of us. Within us lie both sexes, both parts of the division we see reflected outside of us. Yin and Yang.

Peace and harmony in relationships will only come with this harmony within you, and this can only be brought about by unconditional love. Love without conditions; not the co-dependent

ESET

love that operates from a space of lack and therefore need, but the love that says, "I am here, unwavering and constant without need of anything in return, because I am already whole and complete." See yourself as this, and your perception of the world will shift into a place of love and harmony.

The Goddess Kali on Harmony

Harmony always begins with you. It never starts out there. Out there in the world, out there in other people, out there in the nations, out there in your experiences. Harmony out there is always traced back to within you. If you see a bleak, distrustful world, if you see pain in the people around you, find the harmony within. How do you find harmony within? Look inside your heart. Your heart will speak volumes to you about where the source of disharmony is. Ask your heart what hurts and fears it is holding. There may be many and if you have never asked your heart this question, it may not even answer you. It would stand in disbelief that on this day you are choosing to communicate with it, after all these years of never having relationship with it.

Your heart is your centre to the connection of everything outside of you. It is not the eyes that you see with, it is your heart! If you heart has been hurt and you are storing this hurt, your vision will be skewed with pain. If people love you but your heart is holding fear from prior experiences that love equals pain, then you will only feel pain, not love, from your outer experiences.

And then the heart is layered with blame and feelings of injustice and states of unforgiveness. The layers run deep when left unchecked, and the mind continues to try to make a success out of life, tricking you into believing that if only you just obtained this or made enough money, or had enough decent friends or established some credibility in your career. If only the world would change out there, perhaps my heart may not be heavy. Perhaps I would not feel overwhelmed and frustrated with life.

If your heart could speak, it would ask you to listen to its beating, just as the earth has its own heartbeat. Look around you to see what has been happening to your Mother Earth. Her heartbeat has been ignored by many, and she has been destroyed in many ways, but she keeps beating and providing you a home and shelter and keeps supporting you by means of a place to walk on, to travel on. So too does your heart keep on beating, keep supporting you and keep providing you with a home for your soul to reside within your body. Ignoring the earth's heartbeat has not made her a healthy place, nor will ignoring your own heart. Your heart needs to be open in all its glory for you to find harmony.

The heart is full of templates and grids and storage centres where everything is collected and stored from all of your lives. It stores the cellular memory of what you have learnt about love. If you have been told you are loved and then treated in unloving ways, this has caused mistrust and the heart begins to close. There are some that make their way through this life never ever having their hearts be fully open, but this is the time for all hearts to open. The planet cannot survive without its heartbeat, and with these waves of ascension, it will not see you survive without opening your hearts also.

Many have prophesied that there will be those who will not survive the new earth. Many channels have written of mass turmoil on this earth by way of earthquakes and destruction and people dying. Do not be mistaken. The dying that is to occur is only that of the ego and what is no longer working for survival. To continue with closed hearts spells doom. Just as a literally constricted heart is blocked by clogged arteries and vessels, so too is your happiness and harmony blocked by a closed heart.

No pill can give you the deep harmony you seek. There are so many things in your world now that have become artificial. You have artificial grass, artificial parks, artificial friendships via social media, artificial sweetener, artificial beaches – I could go on but I'm sure you get my point. Art-official. The official art of making something false appearing real! The artificial feelings that medications provide can be a temporary solution for a long-term problem that needs to be looked at eventually. The problem of harmony doesn't reside in your brain or mind; your heart is the central place of existence. I'm sure you've heard of the saying, "looking for love in all the wrong places". If you see that money seems to make the world go round but believe love should, why would you believe the art-official response from your experts that the mind and brain need fixing? Wouldn't it make more sense that if love can heal all, the problem resides in the heart?

As a race you have mastered the art of even an art-official heart. The KEY to harmony is to put an end to all the art-official falseness and get real. Stop taking shortcuts to create an illusionary world where you are merely surviving and existing. That's what an art-official heart does; it allows itself to keep beating, giving you the home you need to live, but that's about all. Don't you want to be more, live more, have more passion, and love more? Isn't that what everyone is chasing? Want to stop chasing and have that authentic depth of harmony and love? Go within your heart and listen. Be daring enough to hear its whisper and be attentive to its needs.

Be courageous enough to give love to you and your heart so that you are not dependent on things and other people to provide validation. You need your heart to survive, BUT it also needs YOU! It needs you to forgive yourself where you have been self-critical and in all of the ways you have abused yourself over the years. It needs you to forgive others who have hurt you. It wants you to see that their behaviour towards you was never about your capacity to be loved or your worthiness of love, but rather that their heart had been closed somewhere along the way too. Just as two wrongs don't make a right, two closed hearts don't create another open one. Want to see a world full of love and harmony? Heal the heart within. Let go of all the hurts, pains and injustices, for as you harbour them within, you harbour them without, out 'there' in the world. Same same but different!

*Armed with the Key of Harmony,
it's time to embark on a new
journey into the 13th Key.*

Book 2 Coming Soon

Afterword

Although this book has been about a soul approach to mental health symptoms, and I have discussed trauma in the Key of Consciousness, I wish to add in closing that trauma also produces compartmentalisation, whereby voices may originate not from other worlds but from within this one via the fragmented self. Through my studies and research, I understand these ideas and wholeheartedly support the notion that these voices are also an attempt at self-regulation; a coping mechanism to deal with extreme trauma. It has not been my expertise or my life experience. For an alternate view of this approach of looking at schizophrenia in a supportive, non-symptomology way, I would highly recommend discovering Eleanor Longden, a psychologist who offers her own life experience in her TED talk and in her book, *The Voices in My Head.*

Also, in the spirit of following a holistic framework, I feel it important to mention that there are a myriad of physiological causes of mental health symptoms relating to gut health, the thyroid, and what is known in the bio-medicine field as under-methylation and elevated pyrroles. I have had to address all of these issues at different times and saw a bio-medicine specialist while writing this book. When my results came in, the doctor reported that my pyrrole levels were off the charts. Wondering how I was even still standing, he explained that in the care of a psychiatrist, I would have been diagnosed with severe depression, anxiety and ADHD! The rectification: a specialised dose of vitamins and minerals such as magnesium, zinc and vitamin C specific to my body's needs with no adverse side effects.

Finally, I can't stress enough how important having a sense of humour has been in my own recovery. The ability to laugh at myself and life has been my saving grace above all else. Find something to laugh at every day. Laughing at your mistakes will help you to remember them with joy and not repeat them more than condemnation ever will. You deserve that. I wish you joy and grace on your journey.

Marie
ANTOINETTE

Acknowledgements

To my beautiful mother, a sensitive soul who tells me that my blood is made of light and who continually tells everyone that will listen that 'heaven is coming to the earth'. I know you're not crazy; you're absolutely right and I love you dearly for being one of my greatest teachers.

To my adoring and understanding father, who has never stopped supporting me through all my spiritual crises and has always been my guiding light, who also sees the divinity within me when I cannot. Thank you from the deepest part of my being, and an extra thank you to your mother and her mother for being the gifted healers they also are.

To my four brothers, who have unknowingly taught me and continue to teach me through their experiences that we are all from the family of light on our return journey home. I love you all.

To Maria, my therapist, who continually supported me in not seeing myself through the eyes of pathology, even when I swore to her that I had all the signs and symptoms of being sick. Who taught me to love the child within and put up with my constant ranting through my awakenings of this book needing to come out. After all these years, it's finally here! Thank you and yes, I will remember to breathe and 'go gently' – ha ha.

Thank you to Denise, who taught me so much in my spiritually formative years. You paved a path of enlightenment for me.

Thank you for all the fellow spiritual seekers in recovery who have supported my own path throughout the years. Without your support I wouldn't be here today.

Thank you to Lisa, my divine earth sister and goddess, and my friend and fellow dimensional traveller brother Dan, who assisted me to traverse the intra-dimensions I so needed to, to finally bring this work to fruition. You were my accidental heroes in this unfoldment.

Thank you to Chris, who was there during my final stages of initiation. Without your unwavering support and confirmation that I was undergoing a spiritual transformation, I would not have been able to bounce back and get this book out in record time.

Thank you to my soul brother, Luke, who assisted me in the final stages of this book. Your selfless passion to serve me and the rest of humanity in the highest way has contributed in more ways than you know.

And finally, to my spiritual family and team. Your ongoing guidance, wisdom and teachings act as a bridge to the creator of all that is which resides in all of us. I will continue on, blessed by your guidance and forever being the student and teacher simultaneously.

About the Author

Marie Antoinette was born in Australia to Lebanese and Egyptian parents. She has a background in Gestalt Psychotherapy and Family Constellations and has worked with young people in the areas of addiction, mental health, complex trauma and disability. She has also taught at a tertiary level in the fields of community services, mental health and counselling.

Marie's passion is walking two worlds and helping people to find and live their soul purpose. She is a gifted psychic medium and channeler, and is also a Theta Healing and Crystal Dreaming practitioner. Her various programs and workshops help people to heal on a soul level and raise their own intuitive abilities.

Marie is also a talented speaker and comedian, and incorporates humour into everything she does, with the belief that laughter is the language of the soul and is indeed the best medicine.

www.marieantoinette.co

Facebook pages:

◊   Marie Antoinette

◊   Marie Antoinette – Official

◊   Soul Healing

◊   Marie Antoinette MC & Comedian

Instagram: marieantoinette.co

Recommended Reading List

Eleanor Longden, *Learning from the Voices in My Head,* 2013, TED Conferences

Gwen Olsen, *Confessions of an Rx Drug Pusher,* 2009, Paperback, iUniverse, Paperback edition

Stanislav Grof and Christina Grof, *Spiritual Emergency: When personal transformation becomes a crisis,* 1989, Tarcher Perigee, 1st edition

Peter Breggin and David Cohen, *Your Drug May Be Your Problem,* 2007, Da Capo Press, 1st edition

Dr Erika Schwartz MD and Melissa Jo Peltier, *Don't Let Your Doctor Kill You,* audio book, Post Hill Press

Thomas Szasz, *The Myth of Mental Illness,* 2010, HarperCollins Publishers Inc.

Bruce Lipton, *The Biology of Belief,* 2015, Hay House Inc.

Neale Donald Walsch, *Conversations with God,* 1996, G.P. Putnam's Sons, 1st edition

Dr David R. Hawkins, *Power vs Force*, 2014, Hay House, 2nd edition

Paulo Coelho, *Veronika Decides to Die*, 2006, Harper Perennial, Translation edition

Odette Nightsky, *The Bridge Between Two Worlds*, 1999, Self-published

Nicolya Christi, *2012: A Clarion Call*, 2011, Bear & Company

Raym Richards, *Spirit World: A diary of an urban shaman*, 2017, Global Healing

Byron Katie, *Loving What Is,* 2003, Three Rivers Press, Reprint edition

Dolores Cannon, *The Three Waves of Volunteers and the New Earth*, 2011, Ozark Mountain Pub

Michael Newton, *Destiny of Souls,* 2000, Llewellyn Publications, Subsequent edition

Peter A. Levine, *Waking the Tiger: Healing Trauma*, 2011, North Atlantic, 1st edition

Bessel van der Kolk, *The Body Keeps the Score*, 2015, Penguin Group USA, Reprint edition

Barbara Marciniak, *Bringers of the Dawn: Teachings from the Pleiadians*, 1992, Bear & Company, Original edition

Program Offers

Are you a seeker of knowledge and truth?

Looking for a soul awakening?

Looking to find your purpose and ready to heal those blocks within that are stopping you from manifesting your heart's desires?

Do you want healing that goes beyond the spiritual and into the depths of your soul? Ready to tap into that tree of knowledge within you and make a transformation to shift yourself into gear?

This program offers a deep dive into you and your soul purpose. It involves in-depth healing sessions, and personal and group mentoring designed to provide an inner and outer transformation that removes blocks and helps to raise your intuition, so that you can walk with spirit in your own life and learn to live the path of soul ascension.

As a client in one of my programs, you will be connected to a supportive network and an array of knowledge to support your progress with mentoring as your psychic gifts open and your soul is activated.

To learn more, book your free discovery session:

Email: marie@marieantoinette.co

Subject line: Reader Offer – Free Discovery

Ignition Healing

A transformational healing that starts off with a psychic scan that dives deep into all elements of your being. Through the psychic eye, no stone is left unturned as your future pathway is revealed along with the roadblocks that are causing disharmony. Physical, mental and emotional and spiritual elements are looked into and discussed. An energetic healing is performed to release lower vibrational energies. Thought patterns contributing to self-defeating beliefs are released. A doorway will be opened for any ancestors and guides to enter to assist with your healing. No two healings are ever the same and the healings are instant, with many clients reporting significant and immediate changes in their being.

Value $220. Readers of this book – Investment $99

Email: marie@marieantoinette.co

Subject line: Ignition Healing – Reader Offer

Events

Marie is available to speak at events to share her psychic unfoldment/ mental health journey and speak about soul purpose, overcoming adversity, mental health, the spirit world, ascension, empowerment, consciousness, using humour as a therapeutic tool and taking a soul approach to wellbeing. She is also available to do guest live channellings and, of course, help your audiences be entertained with joy.

Email: marie@marieantoinette.co

Subject line: Speaking Engagement

CPSIA information can be obtained
at www.ICGtesting.com
Printed in the USA
LVHW082359051222
734629LV00016B/1152